MW00353671

THE
TRANSFORMATION

HOW TO USE DIGITAL TRANSFORMATION TECHNOLOGY
TO REDUCE COSTS, ACCELERATE DELIVERY TIMES,
AND PROVIDE EXCEPTIONAL VALUE

RICHARD CATALANO
WITH JOSHUA LEASE

The Transformation: How to Use Digital Transformation Technology to Reduce Costs, Accelerate Delivery Times, and Provide Exceptional Value

By Richard Catalano with Joshua Lease

Published by: Platinum PMO LLC
www.PlatinumPMO.com

ISBN: 978-0-578-61771-8

Copyright ©2019 Richard Catalano. All rights reserved. No part of this publication may be reproduced, distributed, or transmitted in any form or by any means, including photocopying, recording, or other electronic or mechanical methods, without the prior written permission of the publisher, except in the case of brief quotations embodied in critical reviews and certain other noncommercial uses permitted by copyright law. For further information, please contact the author at: richard.catalano@platinumpmo.com

Dedication

I dedicate this book to my amazing family. To my wife, Cheryl, my inspiration of positivity. Thank you for believing in me and unconditionally supporting me to pursue my dream.

To my parents, Rick and Marilyn. Thank you for my life! Thank you for instilling in me an incredible work ethic and a passion to strive to be the best that I can be.

To my children, RJ, Dan, and Lance. What can I say, I tried! In all seriousness, you have been the joy of my life and to watch you grow up to become the men you have become has made me the proudest father of all time!

To my brother, Jeff, my sister-in-law, Melissa, my nephews, Nick and Kyle, my daughter-in-law, Diana, and my grandchildren, Ryder and Freyja. Thank you for all the love and support you have given me throughout the years. I am eternally grateful!

Contents

Acknowlegdments   *vii*

Transformation Introduction   *ix*

Bonus Material   *xi*

//

Chapter 1: The New Program Manager   1

Chapter 2: Family Man   7

Chapter 3: The Guide   11

Chapter 4: Teams   19

Chapter 5: Program Management   33

Chapter 6: Program Plan Structure   43

Chapter 7: The Chain Factory   53

Chapter 8: Problems   67

Chapter 9: The Budget Planning Meeting   71

Chapter 10: Contract Financial Structures   81

Chapter 11: The Selection   87

Chapter 12: Communication Management   93

Chapter 13: The Surgeon   107

////////////////////////////////

Chapter 14: Risk Management   111

Chapter 15: Issues Management   125

Chapter 16: Key Decision Management   133

Chapter 17: Scope and Change Control   143

Chapter 18: Slipping   159

Chapter 19: Recovery   163

Chapter 20: Quality Management   167

Chapter 21: Life Goes On   181

Chapter 22: Knowledge Management   183

Chapter 23: Program Integration   193

Chapter 24: Leadership Principles   203

Chapter 25: Developing Leadership   213

Chapter 26: Implementation   223

Chapter 27: Epilogue   231

Chapter 28: Closing Remarks   239

About Rick Catalano   *243*

Acknowledgments

A book like this would not have been possible without a lifetime of experiences and the clients, mentors, and writers who helped me learn and grow as a professional consultant.

I first want to thank all of my managers and partners from the old Ernst & Young and PricewaterhouseCoopers consulting firms who taught me what it meant and what it took to be a professional IT consultant and project manager. Your guidance and coaching taught me so much in my formative years in this business, and your leadership inspired me to follow in your incredible footsteps.

I would also like to thank my former clients from my formative years who were patient with me through my failures and evolution as a professional and who taught me that if you always do what you think is right in your heart, you cannot go wrong, as well as what it means to be a servant leader.

I would like to posthumously thank Dr. Eliyahu Goldratt for his teachings surrounding the theory of constraints and critical chain project management and the dozens of other authors who have helped formulate my philosophies in program leadership and management. They were game changers in my critical thinking and approach to helping deliver excellence to my clients.

Lastly, this book would not have happened without the support of my friends and collaborators, Ben Bennett and Joshua Lease. Thank you both for your encouragement, honest feedback, and providing your invaluable skills in structuring and guiding me throughout the process of bringing this book to life.

Transformation Introduction

Ask a hundred people, "What is digital transformation?" and you will probably get a hundred different answers. Google it and you will get over 318 million responses. For the purposes of this book, we define digital transformation as: "the integration of digital technology into all areas of your business, fundamentally changing how you operate, while embracing a culture of innovation and delivering exemplary value to your customers. This reimagining of business in the digital age is digital transformation.

Digital transformation is *big business*! As of the writing of this book, researchers are projecting that digital transformation will be a 2.2 trillion-dollar industry by 2022 with a compounding annual growth rate (CAGR) between 15-20 percent. The strategy consulting market for digital transformation—represented by the likes of McKinsey, Boston Consulting Group, A.T. Kearny, and Accenture—is predicting a 40 billion dollar market place in the USA alone by 2025 with a CAGR over 7 percent. And that is just the strategy work!

Digital transformations are expansive programs that change the landscapes of companies and can make or break their future. However, there is a dark side to the industry that does not garner as much attention, and that is the pain that companies go through in implementing these transformations.

According to research, more than 65 percent of digital transformation implementations today are either over budget, delivered late, and/or don't deliver the value for which they were originally intended and forecasted. These typical pains are costing companies billions of dollars in overages, and in some cases (17 percent), threaten the existence of the entire company.

Ladies and gentlemen, the stakes are high!

But the payoff is potentially even greater. Done well, a digital transformation will reduce costs, build efficiencies, and allow companies to better manage their assets—just to name a few of the many benefits. A company that undergoes a well-executed transformation can take or regain market share, reach untapped markets, better serve customers, and add value to existing customers and shareholders.

After decades of successfully consulting with Fortune 500 companies, the team at Platinum PMO has developed procedures, practices, methodologies, and a digital transformation implementation platform (called AMIGO) that are beneficial to the transformation process from inception to implementation and build the connections for a successful implementation from the C-suite to ground level.

We wrote this book to give you a helping hand both in understanding the "story" of a digital transformation and to provide tools and a framework for understanding the underlying processes that we have learned from decades in the industry. We chose to embed the principles and techniques you need for a successful implementation in a compelling story with interesting characters. It holds your attention while you experience the process through the eyes of a new program manager, Mike Bennett, who is on a profound professional and personal journey.

Join Mike as he learns from an expert consultant and grows into a leader able to guide the company—and his family—through a transformation.

Bonus Material

As a special thank you for purchasing this book, we wanted to provide you with some additional materials that could help jumpstart your own digital transformation efforts with your company. As you are reading through the book and looking for some deeper insights, please go to our website at:

www.platinumpmo.com/thetransformationbook

Download these free complimentary materials containing exclusive key checklists, graphics, and additional bonus material not found in the book.

Thanks again and enjoy *The Transformation!*

CHAPTER 1

The New Program Manager

Michael Bennett walked into the waiting room in Charles Offerman's office and was immediately struck by how his boss (or his high-priced decorator) had mastered the idea of minimal industrialist. Everything screamed restrained class, from the carpet to the few wall decorations beneath their individualized lights.

Offerman's personal assistant, Shirley Fomby, sat behind a modern granite-and-glass desk with no fewer than three monitors, and as Mike stepped out of the elevator and into the waiting area, she smiled warmly and stopped typing.

"Mr. Bennett," Shirley said. "Mr. Offerman will be with you in a moment. Can I offer you some water?"

Mike nodded. Offerman talked about his water often; he owned one of those expensive ionizers that changed the water's pH value so it tasted extra smooth and apparently could cure everything from eczema to cancer. The older man swore by the stuff, said it would keep him young. Mike just liked the way it tasted and sipped it slowly from an expensive crystal glass.

After just a few sips, Offerman opened his office door and stepped out. "Mike!" he said happily, coming to shake his employee's hand.

Entering the early part of his later years, Offerman was a reasonably fit man with thinning, close-trimmed hair and a once-broad chest that his perfectly tailored suit made you think hadn't settled around his middle. (Having seen him in his cycling gear, Mike knew differently.) But Offerman did cut the perfect figure of a successful CIO for Extron Energy.

"Mike," he said again, pumping Mike's hand and beginning to draw him back into his office. "Come on back. We've got some big things to discuss—big things."

Like the waiting area, the office as minimal as possible. Everything was spare, dominated by glass and stone. A few awards and a couple of models commemorating Offerman's successes with the company were placed strategically. Instead of looking at the decorations, though, Mike's eyes were immediately drawn to the windows, which dominated two walls and looked out over the beautiful Arkansas River and the city skyline of Little Rock, Arkansas.

Offerman settled himself into a leather office chair that seemed to float on thin metal struts. He gestured to Mike to seat himself in one of the two chairs on the other side of his large desk.

"Mike, I just want you to know before we begin that I put the utmost trust in you—I hope you know that." Mike had suspected that Offerman had marked him for a fast track after the Workseam Project had gone so well, but it was nice to have the CIO tell him that to his face.

Offerman went on, "I've had my eye on you since you knocked it out of the park on the Workseam Initiative, and I think you're my guy for something else—something new. This is a career-maker, Mike."

"Thank you for your vote of confidence, Mr. Offerman," Mike replied.

Offerman waved him off. "Call me Charles, Mike. We're going to be doing a lot of amazing things together, and 'Mr. Offerman' is going to get really cumbersome really fast."

First-name basis with the boss—nice, he thought.

"So," Mike managed, "what are these 'amazing things' we're going to be doing together, Charles?" It felt like he was tasting the use of Offerman's first name like a new flavor—and he liked it. It tasted like success.

"How familiar are you with digital transformations?" Charles asked.

Mike thought for a moment. "They're ambitious," he replied carefully.

"Done right, they can take a company to another level—or reclaim lost market share."

Charles nodded thoughtfully, fingers steepled. "Right," he agreed. "Done wrong—" He let the idea hang in the air for a moment. "Done wrong, they can go way over budget, even bankrupt a company. McKinsey and Oxford University recently did a study of 3,600 IT-enabled transformation programs with budgets greater than 15 million and found that 65 percent of these programs were over budget, and 33 percent of them went over schedule and provided 56 percent less value than originally chartered to deliver. They said the cost overrun for these programs totals 66 *billion* dollars. Absolutely staggering!"

The CIO leaned back in his chair and puffed out a pent-up breath through his lips like he was trying to whistle. "Of the 65 percent of the projects that had overruns, 25 percent had overruns greater than 50 percent, with an average of a 78 percent cost overrun. And, worst yet, 17 percent of these programs went so badly that it threatened the existence of their organizations."

Mike was aware that American Grid's disastrous implementation had made national headlines. Then there was Western Electric & Gas, which was in bankruptcy due to fires and explosions that could possibly have been prevented if they had the right digital technologies in place.

"Here's the deal," Charles went on. "We *have to* do this. We're losing out in some key areas—which I think you know. From a customer perspective, we need to take another look at our value proposition and identify new ways to add value for our existing customers and connect our brand to new customers who are looking for alternative energy suppliers. We need to do a better job of reducing costs and building efficiencies in our supply chain. We also need to get better controls on our assets. We need to be able to know exactly where every piece of equipment is throughout our geography. We need to be able to better predict when maintenance needs to occur and actually fix problems before they happen. We cannot have a WE&G situation here—it could kill the company."

He leaned forward, looking at Mike intently. "When I told you I trust you, I wasn't just blowing smoke. I do. You're smart, you're driven, and you've got the background for this." Charles paused for a heartbeat. "Let's just be honest. Mac Powel is not a good fit for this initiative. He is nearing retirement, and it could take years to finish our vision. Besides, if we put him in this role today, he'd pull out what little hair he has left," Charles said with a sheepish smile. "Mike, I want *you* to head up the transformation."

Mike stopped breathing for a moment, or maybe time had stopped. Offerman—Charles—wasn't kidding; this was a career-maker.

Or breaker.

Sixty-five percent went over budget? Seventeen percent threatened the existence of the entire company?

A flood of emotions and thoughts swirled through Mike in that brief moment. Excitement, fear, dismay. The possibilities rattled through his head—working with the CIO, being his guy for the transformation, would position Mike like nothing else. He could be in line to follow Offerman as the CIO; he'd said himself that Mac, one of Charles' senior directors, was not the right fit for this initiative. Charles could be grooming Mike as a possible successor.

But 65 percent? That's a lot of failures, a lot of overruns. Mike knew he was smart—it's why he got into IT and was placed so highly at Extron. He'd excelled at everything he'd done there, from the Workseam Project Charles had mentioned to a dozen smaller projects he'd been a part of.

But this was different. This was a whole other level. Succeed or fail, there would be no going back from this one. Everyone's job could hang on how well he did at this. The looming stats of failure seemed like an abyss opening beneath him.

The bright lure of the possibilities, however, was greater than the dark threat of failure, and Mike could feel himself abort a deep dive into insecurity and fear and start heading up toward what it would mean for him—and for his family—if he pulled this off. After all, he knew Extron from the inside as only someone who'd come up fresh from school could. He had relationships, knew the systems inside and out, and apparently had the support of the CIO himself.

He realized he hadn't said anything. While time for him may have stopped, for Charles, it was moving at normal speed.

"I'm honored, sir," Mike finally managed to say.

A big grin split his boss's weathered face. "Like I said, Mike, call me Charles, and I've seen the look in your eyes plenty of times before," Charles said.

He came around the desk and casually sat on its edge. "You're excited, but you're scared as hell, too, right?"

It was that obvious? Mike just nodded.

Charles barked a laugh. "I've probably had that look on my own face a time or two. I get it—it's a lot of pressure. You've done well, Mike, and like I said, I trust you. I need you to be the guy on the ground on this, running it, leading it, having the energy to make it happen." He took another drink. "But there's a lot riding on this—I don't have to tell you that. There'll be a lot of pressure, and let's be honest, you've never done anything like this before."

Thanks for reminding me, Mike thought.

Charles continued, "That's why you won't be in this alone. I've already called an old friend named Jonas Romano, and trust me, you're going to love him. He consulted with Tuterro Energy on their transformation last year, and I happen to know that he helped them get through on budget and deal with some of the challenges they experienced working with their system integrators."

"He was at Tuterro?"

Charles grunted. "Yeah—Mark Steinson over there and I are on the same charity golf team, and he happened to brag about it to me over drinks a while back. Mentioned Jonas—probably didn't know we go way back. Anyway, if he can bring those idiots at Tuterro through whole, I figure that he can probably help us succeed with flying colors. With you taking point and Jonas to back you up, I think we can really do this thing right."

He seemed so confident that it buoyed Mike up, too. Suddenly, the doubts he'd had earlier seemed like distant, unimportant memories.

Charles mentioned, "The first phase of this digital transformation will require us to lay down a solid foundation of leading practices and cloud computing capabilities throughout our marketing, customer, supply chain, and asset management process areas. We'll also need to take advantage of the incredible technology advancements available in the utilities space surrounding big data, artificial intelligence, and the 'Internet of Things.' Our short-list of software applications that will provide us that foundation has been whittled down to Salesforce.com for the marketing, sales, and customer relationship aspects, and SAP for just about everything else. Given our current internal skills gap with these applications and understanding of what is possible with the newer capabilities around IoT, big data, and AI, we are going to need some help. We are going to need to bring in a firm or two who know the ins and outs of the utilities space and that can help us reimagine energy for the next century."

Mike nodded; that made sense.

Offerman went on, "As part of this, we are going to need to build out a robust request for proposal that identifies what we are looking to do, our initial scope, their qualifications, and why we should choose their services. At the same time, we should start doing our own homework on what we think our detailed scope is going to be and start gathering intelligence and documentation on our current processes, systems, data, and integrations as these will be important."

"I can definitely do that," Mike said as Charles paused.

"Finally, I want you to work with Jonas for his independent thoughts on how we should structure this initiative from a program governance perspective. I know we are going to get some suggestions from our vendors, but I want an independent perspective on how this structure can be sustained after our vendors leave and our organization is driving the transformation's evolution. I also want you guys to start building a budget on what you think this is going to cost us 'all in.' It's been my experience that the numbers we get as part of the RFP are usually on the low side and usually don't consider our internal costs very well. Again, work with Jonas on this as well, as he has done this on other projects."

Charles finished his drink and then rattled the ice cubes around in his glass absentmindedly, maybe getting lost in his own thoughts for a moment. Mike still had half of his glass left.

"We can do this, Mike. I believe in you. I know Jonas, and I hear he has some experience with some amazing software to help govern and facilitate communication on large-scale initiatives like the one we are about to start. He says that's one of the most important things—getting all the separate pieces to play nicely with each other and talk to each other. We should definitely evaluate this software, and if we think it would be a good fit for what we are doing, then we should build it into our budget."

He had a twinkle in his eye as he leaned forward, ending the meeting with his body language. "Let's just say that it could become your new 'best friend.'"

CHAPTER 2

Family Man

Mike drove home after work without remembering much of what he did between the time he finished talking to Charles Offerman and when he pulled into his driveway. He was on autopilot, his mind on his upcoming task as Extron's newly-appointed Program Director of their largest digital transformation ever.

As he pulled his Lexus into the garage, his thoughts finally snapped to the present as he narrowly avoided running over his son's bike, which was left in the middle of the garage. Normally, this would be enough to make him angry as he walked in the door, but he was still too buoyed up by his news to let this pull him down.

Mike was excited to tell his wife, Nancy, about his promotion. She'd supported him through all the difficulties during his career, and now he felt like that faith in him was paying off. He couldn't wait to tell her the good news.

Mike knew he was a passionate guy, and he had a great relationship with Nancy. She was one of the few people in the world he felt he could be completely open with. They'd been married five years, and each of them had brought children into the relationship from their previous marriages.

Mike and Nancy met in an unusual way under unusual circumstances. A year or so after Mike's divorce, he finally got around to decorating his house to make it a little "warmer" and inviting to his two boys Donny and MJ, or Michael Junior. The younger, Donny, was diagnosed with autism spectrum disorder right before his third birthday, and MJ, the eldest, was diagnosed with ADHD at the age of four and was as high-energy as they come, creating hurdles all his own. The two of them together were a force to be reckoned with.

Though divorces are almost never pretty, when it came to the children, there was a fair and balanced relationship between Mike and his ex, and they worked through a 50/50 custody agreement, so Mike got to be with the kids a lot.

One Saturday, when the boys were six and seven, Mike threw on a t-shirt and sweat pants, his typical weekend attire, and carted the kids to a home decorating store to look at wallpaper samples for their rooms. As Mike was browsing the dozens of samples, the kids were in rare form, terrorizing the customers and employees.

He was tapped on the shoulder by a beautiful blonde woman. She asked, "Do these two belong to you? They were found in the bedding department wrestling on the beds and using them as trampolines." Although this was typical behavior for his children, Mike appeared shocked and embarrassed as if this had never happened before.

"My most sincere apologies, Nancy," he said, looking at her nametag. "I'm not sure what's gotten into them this morning! I'll make sure they stay by my side from now on."

Nancy just smiled and said, "It's okay. It happens more than you can imagine."

A few minutes later, Mike's decorator re-appeared, and he asked her about Nancy. His decorator mentioned she was a single mother of an eight-year-old daughter, Gabriella. Mike was kind of excited to hear that news, but then he immediately became depressed when he realized that he just met the woman of his dreams while unshaven and wearing a sweat-stained t-shirt, weathered sweat pants, and a ballcap—while being responsible for the two barbarians who were wreaking havoc in bedding.

During Mike's future visits to the store, he was always properly dressed and well-groomed in hopes of seeing Nancy. After a few months, he finally got the nerve to ask her out, and she accepted. A few months later, he asked for her hand in marriage, and she accepted again. And the rest, as they say, is history.

Mike was ready to tell her all about what had happened at work, but he found an unexpected setting when he came home. Nancy was seated on the couch, arms folded tightly over her chest, and face in a scowl. Gabbi was standing in front of her, nearly bristling, her posture tight and defensive, face red.

"I don't want to talk about it!" Gabbi growled.

"Well, we *are* talking about it," Nancy countered, not shifting. "From the moment I found it in your purse, we were *going* to talk about it."

"You shouldn't even be searching my things!" Gabbi shot back. "That's my property—it's *private*!"

Nancy was nonplussed. "Honey, I wasn't searching your things—it fell off the counter and everything came out. Including this." She held up a package that she'd been holding tightly in her fist. "You told me you were clean."

Gabbi almost flinched, like seeing the drugs somehow made it all more real than when they were out of sight. Unconvincingly, she mumbled, "It's not even mine."

"Really? We're going to go there?" Nancy deadpanned. She looked up, saw Mike for the first time, and realized it wasn't a private conversation. Gabbi turned and saw Mike too, her face flushing with embarrassment.

"I'm sorry," Mike said, not quite sure how to handle being in the middle of this. "I heard raised voices..."

Gabbi said, "Great, now you can both beat up on me."

At the same time, Nancy rolled over her with, "It's okay, this involves you too."

Gabbi was going silent, shutting down, and she flung herself onto the couch. Gabbi and Mike had always gotten along well. They were different enough to be into separate things, but alike enough to not rub each other the wrong way often. He'd been in her life since she was eight, and really, he was the only father she'd known most of her life since her dad wasn't in the picture.

It had pained the both of them to see her struggle with drugs early in her teens. This wasn't the first time, and Mike feared that Gabbi didn't have a healthy sense of her own mortality—she seemed like she'd try anything, no matter the risk.

"I found this when her purse fell off the counter," Nancy said, holding out the little white bag. Mike walked forward and took it. He'd had wilder days in college, and he recognized the contents.

"Bring on the double team," Gabbi muttered.

Mike looked back and forth between them. Nancy started to open her mouth, but Mike jumped in just a little quicker. "I think we all need to take a break, cool down. We're not going to get anywhere in the heat of the moment."

Gabbi looked like he'd thrown her a lifeline, then smothered it beneath a blanket of "angry teen." Nancy opened her mouth again and then closed it. She frowned and then, at last, nodded. "All right. But this isn't going to go away, Gabbi. I'll see you for dinner in an hour, and we'll talk about this later tonight. You remember what I said last time?"

Gabbi was silent for a moment until she realized Nancy hadn't meant that rhetorically. "I don't need rehab," she muttered back.

"We'll talk about it later. I love you, and I'm not going to let you do this to yourself."

For a moment, Gabbi seemed torn between continuing the fight and the lure of being allowed to leave the room. Maybe wondering if the offer might be too good to be true, after a moment's hesitation, she bolted for her room. Nancy looked over at Mike, her face still clouded and angry.

"I thought—I'd *hoped* she could stay clean," she murmured. "But now I know. What are we going to do?"

Mike sat down beside her, news about his job forgotten. "We'll figure it out," he said, putting his arm around Nancy. "Together."

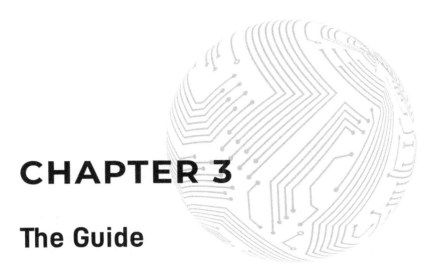

CHAPTER 3

The Guide

Mike's morning was a blur of emails and list-making of all of the things he needed to transition off of his current plate so he can start focusing on his new role. During this process, his desk phone rang. Mike picked up.

"Mr. Bennett?" It was Charles Offerman's assistant, Shirley. "Mr. Offerman wonders if you have the time to come up to his office."

"Now?"

"Yes," she replied as though it should've been obvious. "If that's not inconvenient," she added as an afterthought that seemed to imply that she had no doubt that it *would* be convenient—or he'd better make it that way.

Mike headed up, and this time when he got to Charles' office, the door was opened. The assistant ushered him right in to find Charles sitting on one side of his desk, and another man, slightly younger, was sitting in one of the two chairs on the opposite side.

Even seated, Mike could tell Jonas was a tall guy, and he had graying dark hair and glasses. He had a calm confidence about him, as though he weren't out of place here in the CIO's office drinking the dark, rich coffee from Offerman's gourmet espresso maker. His suit was nice without being obviously expensive, and he had a friendly smile that put Mike immediately at ease.

"Jonas, I'd like you to meet Mike," Charles said. The other man stood—yep, tall—and gave Mike a good, firm handshake and genuine smile.

Jonas said, "Charles tells me good things about you. I hear we're going to be working together."

"Ah, thanks... I fake it well," Mike deflected.

"Mike, please, join us," Charles urged. Mike sat, and Charles went on, "Jonas is one of the top SAP transformation consultants around. I've known him for years."

"I hear you really helped Tuterro," Mike offered.

Jonas nodded modestly. "Yeah, that's why they pay me the big bucks!"

Charles seemed pleased as he looked across his desk at Mike and Jonas. "I feel really good about this," he intoned, crossing his arms over his chest and leaning back in his chair. "I'm going to set you guys free to carry on without me. Get to know each other; you'll be working together *a lot*. Go grab coffee or drinks or something."

With those instructions, Mike and Jonas left Offerman's office and agreed to meet up in half an hour at the local SheBrews Coffee—a little boutique cafe that had held Starbucks at bay with amazing coffee, which they ground and roasted in-house, and an assortment of baked goods and sandwiches that made it a favorite for those at Extron.

"So, Charles tells me you're his guy," Jonas said after they sat down together. Mike smiled, a little embarrassed yet proud his boss would speak well of him. "What kind of work have you done so far?"

Mike thought for a moment. "Well, I graduated with a double-major in business administration and computer science and joined Extron right out of college as programmer/analyst," he replied. "I spent my first few years supporting a lot of the applications around here and learning about how they all work together. I then got to work on bunch of new software initiatives, first few as a programmer, but then I got promoted to lead analyst on the next couple. Then I got promoted to team lead on the next couple, then to project manager on the next few. After a few big successes, I was offered to run the Workseam Initiative, which was a pretty big deal at the time. And, as they say, the rest is history. Can you tell me a little about yourself?"

Jonas took a drink of his coffee. "Well, after fifteen years of working what used to be known as 'the Big 8,' then 'the Big 6,' and finally 'the Big 4' consulting firms, I decided to put out my own shingle and start my own practice about ten years ago. I'm the proud founder of Transforma Initiative, a consulting company helping organizations implement their digital transformation initiatives. I've been helping companies like Extron and other Fortune 500 industry leaders jumpstart implementation success for over twenty-five years now."

His easy, laid-back manner put Mike at ease, and it was comforting to hear that he had so much experience. "I guess you've helped utilities do this before, since you helped Tuterro," Mike said.

"Oh yeah," Jonas replied with a quick laugh. "I've worked in a variety of industries, including consumer and industrial products, oil and gas, utilities, and publishing spanning the entire value chain."

"So, can you tell me more about what this actually looks like? I've got to admit, I've never done this before," Mike said a little sheepishly.

"You know, Mike," Jonas replied, "very few ever have. I almost always work with companies doing their first transformation—only the vendors have usually done it before. And me, of course."

Mike thought for a moment. "So, this may be a dumb question, but what exactly do you do?"

Jonas smiled, "It's not a dumb question. I give you the strategies I feel will put you in the positive category of digital transformation implementations that are on-time, on-budget, and meet objectives."

"But how do you *do* that?"

"You have probably heard in the past that programs focus on people, process, and technologies?"

Mike nodded.

"Well, the way I look at it, successful programs focus on a couple more things: people, process, technology, DATA, and governance. Now, these components are critical for program success, but they need a set of fundamentals to orchestrate the nuances among these components and enable them to work in harmony. With me so far?"

"Like a common foundation, right?"

"Exactly," Jonas confirmed. "I have eight fundamentals that enable the 'core' to operate successfully: organization and resources; communications management; project planning and tracking; budget planning and cost management; risks, issues, and key decisions; scope management; knowledge retention; and quality control. I'm going to help you understand these and how to use them to help your transformation process be successful."

It was a lot to take in. "Can you tell me a little about them to help me understand?"

"Definitely. We can get into the details another time, but I can give you the broad strokes. Organization and resources is about the traditional types of resources and teams you will need. I can help you with some strategies on how to best organize your resources so you'll have a smooth-running operating rhythm. When we get into project planning and tracking, we'll talk more about strategies for structuring your program plan for consistent measurement. I can help you build a massive integrated program plan in hours instead of weeks. I'll show you how to use the *integrated RACI approach* to maximize the value from all resources on your digital transformation."

"RACI?"

"You know, who's responsible, who's accountable, who needs to be consulted, who needs to be informed. Except, I usually take a few steps further than most places I've seen and have coined the phrase 'integrated RACI.' Through an integrated RACI approach, you can really pinpoint the actual individuals who need to be engaged on every aspect of your program and what their roles are in that engagement. It really helps streamline the communications and hold people accountable for the things they need to deliver.

"When you understand how the integrated RACI can help you, you'll better understand *program bottlenecks*, too, and I will share with you some strategies to help you avoid or manage through these bottlenecks using a project planning technique called *critical chain project planning*."[1]

"I know a little about that," Mike said. "There's a whole science behind the

---

1 Please visit **www.platinumpmo.com/thetransformationbook** to access the prep kit to learn more about critical chain project planning

critical chain technique and how it can be used in traditional waterfall method-ologies or the newer agile methodologies."

"Good!" Jonas said, grinning.

Mike asked, "So which is better? The old waterfall or the newer agile methodologies?"

Jonas laughed. "Both!" he declared. "I'll talk to you about what I call the 'watergile.' We'll get to all that."

"So, what's next after project planning again?"

"Budget planning and cost management. It'll help you leverage data from your project plan to build the initial budgets of your program."

"Like estimating expenses for resources and non-resources?"

Jonas nodded. "See, you understand more of this than you think you do. Tracking your budget and the interrelationships between your plan and your budget, forecasting your remaining budget, and all the financial statistics you need to measure how well your program is financially performing are all so important."

Mike said, "If it starts getting squirrelly, hopefully you can see it happening."

Jonas nodded. "If more companies would do a better job of measuring how much work they have gotten done based on the money they spent already, and then continually updated their forecasts on what it's going to take to get the rest of it completed, they would have a much better picture of what their final financial outcome is going to look like. They then could take the necessary steps and either change behavior to further accelerate their outcomes, make some tough decisions on scope, or prepare their organizations for future cost overruns."

"So scope management," Mike prompted. "Is that scope creep and all that?"

Jonas finished his coffee. "Yes, but first, I like to go over techniques for defining scope—in particular, leveraging your scope definition with the compo-nents in your program plan. But, yes, scope creep and strategies to avoid it are part of it. I also like to go through our entire change control process and how this process can be leveraged to manage and control your program's scope. When we talk about risks, issues, and key decisions, I like to go over a set of governance processes known as 'RAID' or risk, actions, issues, and decisions. There are key differences among those processes, and it's important to know how to properly classify risks vs. issues, issues vs. decisions, and actions vs. decisions."

"What's next?"

"Quality management."

Mike made a sour face. "So how am I supposed to ensure good quality management if I've never seen the process before?"

"I'll help you with key components to monitor during the program, show you the typical components of a quality review, and walk you through the quality control process. Another element that you are going to have to master is knowledge management, because this is where it's easy for those who have become over-reliant on their vendors to realize that they don't know what to do when they're gone. There are tools to capture, facilitate, and maintain program knowledge from the first day of your initiative through the retirement of your digital product and beyond."

Jonas went on, "Every project has its own operating rhythm, and there are techniques you can use to help establish and manage yours."

"You make it sound so easy," Mike replied, finishing his own coffee. "Maybe you should be the program director."

"No," Jonas said easily, leaning back. "That's you. You're about to learn program leadership at a whole new level, and I'll be there to assist every step of the way with some time-tested leadership principles I learned when I was once in your place. These principles will help you get the most out of your people and the most value for your program, and they're things you need in your tool-kit, because I think we both hope that this isn't your ceiling; it's your floor."

"I'm glad you and Offerman are so confident."

Jonas smiled. "Charles wouldn't have picked you if he didn't think you're up to it. But *you* have to think you're up to it, too, Mike."

Mike nodded. "I do. I...I just... How do you balance all this and home? I mean, if I just lived at work, I have no doubt in my mind that I can do the work we need to do for this to be a success. But how do you juggle work and home? I'm a husband and dad, too."

"I know the feeling," Jonas admitted. "My kids are grown and gone now.

And there's no doubt that there were times I'm sure I was gone too much. It's a tough call, Mike, but it is also a very personal call to make. When I was your age, I used to feel guilty as all hell. My peers were working seventy-to-eighty hours a week while I was only working fifty-to-sixty. And at home, I was often too distracted or too tired to fully engage with my wife and children. One nagging voice in my head told me I have to be a better employee or risk career failure; another told me to be a better husband and father or risk failing my family. I wished that at least one of the voices would shut up."

Mike was thinking of his conversation with Nancy as Jonas said this.

Jonas went on, "What I came to realize was that I was hooked on thoughts and feelings that just repeated over and over. I had to somehow break out of that cycle and make a change to how I was thinking. I started labeling my thoughts and feelings on the matter and accepting them for what they were—thoughts and feelings. I tried not acting on every thought or resigning myself to all the negativity, but instead I responded to my emotions with an open attitude, paying attention to them and letting myself experience them.

"The important thing I learned was to show myself some compassion and examine the reality of the situation. What's going on—both internally and externally? When you unhook yourself from your difficult thoughts and emotions, you expand your choices. You can decide to act in a way that aligns with your values. Is my response going to serve me and my organization in the long term as well as the short term? Am I taking a step toward being the leader I most want to be and living the life I most want to live? The mind's thought stream flows endlessly, and emotions change like the weather, but values can be called on at any time, in any situation."

Mike had heard of some of this before and had attended some team-building processes where they used neural-linguistic programming, and what Jonas said reminded him of that.

"When I considered my values," Jonas said, "I recognized how deeply committed I was to both my family and my work; I loved being with my wife and children, but I also cared passionately about leading others through challenging endeavors. So, I resolved to be guided by my principles. I recognized how important it was to get home for dinner with my family every evening when I was in town and to resist work interruptions during that time. But I also had to go out of town often, which sometimes coincided with school events that I would have preferred to attend. Confident that my values—not solely my emotions—were guiding me, I finally found peace and fulfillment."

"Wow," was all Mike could say.

Jonas smiled a sudden, funny smile. "I know, that was a pretty deep share for our first encounter. But I wanted to let you know you are not alone on this. We all go through this."

Mike had no idea how important that was going to be. "Man, Jonas, I'm glad you're in this with me."

Jonas got up, ready to head out. "This is your adventure, Mike. I'm just the guide. But whatever I can do to help, I'll do. But you'll provide the drive. Only you can be the dad your kids need and the husband your wife needs. When it comes to the transformation, though—*that* I can help you with."

Mike stood up, and they walked out together. He already had the feeling that Jonas was a friend—a mentor—even though he hardly knew him. He thought of all the older man had highlighted, all the components they'd be covering together. It seemed so overwhelming, but he got the feeling he really *did* have what it takes.

I guess there's one way to find out, Mike told himself as they left the coffee shop.

CHAPTER 4

Teams

Mike was getting names and information on the team members he would have at his disposal. They were pulling some of the top people from various departments all over the company to spearhead the initiative, but right now, he was simply overloaded by the flood of names, bios, and specialties.

A few names were jumping to the top, recommended by superiors, or championed by one silo or another for their own purposes. Mike didn't know some of the people personally, others just by reputation, but he knew many of the names. Chet Osborn was one of them—a guy Mike had worked with before. Chet was intelligent, could be pretty aggressive, and had once been on a similar trajectory to Mike himself—before his demeanor caused a personnel problem with people below him. Chet's raw potential could make him a real asset, but his reputation also told Mike he might be more trouble than he was worth.

Another name he knew was Gina Paterno, a woman he had worked with on the Workseam Project. Mike liked Gina; she was smart, had good intentions, and was generally well-liked. But she could also be a little slow to make decisions and adapt to new situations. He wasn't sure how well she would do since the whole transformation initiative was by definition new.

"How you organize your teams can help you determine how you use your resources," Jonas explained. He and Mike were walking side-by-side through the Extron building about a week after their time in the coffee shop. Mike's workload had started shifting as he reassigned most of his prior work commitments and started shifting the majority of his daily efforts to his new role and began the planning.

Mike and Jonas had been talking about the importance of getting off to a well-ordered start. "That's the first item of your integrated core, isn't it?" Mike verified. They hadn't really talked about it specifically since, but Jonas had already begun proving himself very valuable. His presence was stabilizing, and he was quickly becoming a friend as well.

"Exactly," Jonas confirmed. "Organization and resources is one of the fundamentals that you will use to successfully drive our digital transformation initiative all the way to completion."

"Do you have any tips on how to get all the data organized?"

"When setting up a digital transformation, I typically look for seven core organizational areas: process teams, technology teams, data teams, organization transformation teams, program leadership team, advisory council, and steering committee team. You don't get to pick the advisory council and steering committee team of business process owners, executive stakeholders, the program sponsor, and other executive-level members. So, I always suggest starting with what you have the most say over."

Together, they entered Mike's office, which had become a de facto meeting place for him and Jonas. "So business process teams first? Why them first?"

"Well, traditionally speaking, there is usually a knee jerk reaction that your digital transformation is 'just another IT project' if it is sponsored by the CIO, but nothing could be further from the truth. Digital transformations are not IT implementations."

"Is that why Charles was saying that Arthur Jonesborough is going to be the program sponsor?" Mike asked. Mike didn't really know the CFO, Jonesborough, but Charles said he was one of the driving forces behind the transformation.

Jonas nodded. "Definitely. This will avoid a lot of problems within the company." Mike got them both a bottle of water from his mini fridge. Jonas opened it and took a drink before continuing.

"As you define your program's charter and scope, you'll see how the options determine which processes are in scope for your program. So far, from what I have gathered, some key strategic objectives need to be accomplished with this program. From a customer perspective, we need to relook at our value proposition and identify new ways to add value for our existing customers and connect our brand to new customers who are looking for alternative energy suppliers. This looks like there are opportunities to re-envision the market-to-opportunity process to connect our brand to new and existing customers as well as the meter-to-cash process, along with our smart grid upgrade and Internet of Things integrations, to enhance the overall experience a customer has in dealing with Extron. There are great opportunities to engage with customers on a whole new level to not only enhance their personal portal experience on your website, but even going so far as to send individuals text messages for power outage updates and real-time messaging on off-peak and peak energy usage. We can even automatically run their dishwashers and washing machines at the correct times of day where energy supply is high and demand is low, thereby lowering the customer's energy consumption costs.

"From a supply chain perspective, we need to do a better job of reducing costs and building efficiencies throughout the entire supply chain. That's typically looking for opportunities in your procure-to-pay processes, including vendor management, product/materials management, transportation management, and warehouse/facilities management. There are some great opportunities in the world of artificial intelligence to allow Extron to optimize its inventory to save the company hundreds of millions of dollars in inventory costs. We will need to investigate a little further if there are other nuggets of opportunity in the supply chain that can help bring value to the organization and satisfy leadership's strategic objectives.

"If I recall, the final objective was the need to get better controls on our assets. We need to be able to know exactly where every piece of equipment is throughout our geography. We also need to be able to better predict when maintenance is required on each piece of equipment and actually fix problems *before* they happen. This will most likely require a complete overhaul of our enterprise asset management processes, as well as developing AI-driven predictive analytics capabilities that will allow us to perform big data computations on each and every smart part sensor you have on each piece of equipment, along with its corresponding functional location coordinates, across your entire geography."

"So, who do you suggest we put on these teams?"

"Well, there are various business process team roles: the process owner—an individual who is in senior leadership who owns the business process for your entire organization.

"Business process team leads—the person who is the on the ground day-to-day leader of your business process. They are responsible for defining and delivering the new business processes in their area for the organization.

"Business sub-process team leads—these are the people assigned by the business process lead to lead the design and development of the sub-processes within the core business process. The scope of a business process is pretty wide, and because of the level of granularity you need to run your organization, you have to break it down into more manageable components. There are a variety of ways to break down your sub-processes within your process area. In my experience, I usually see anywhere from three to six subprocess leads within a business process.

"Business process analysts—now, your business process analysts traditionally report into your business subprocess team leads. These are the people that you pull from the business who have a solid understanding of how the business operates and have what I call a functional/technical acumen. In other words, they understand something about process, how process flows work, how data flows through the processes, and they also know a little bit about the current technology and the systems used to make the processes work in your organization's current state.

"These resources (as well as your subprocess leads and process lead) should be the 'top shelf' resources in your organization for their process area because these are the folks that you're putting in the driver's seat to define your company's future vision for their process area. They are the ones who will be driving the transformation to their peer group once you are ready to go live.

"By the way, the business process analysts, subprocess team leads, and process lead should be dedicated *full time* to your program."

Mike nodded. "That's why we're pulling them from their current roles and back-filling with the temps, right?"

"Exactly," Jonas confirmed. "They need to be able to focus on the task at hand—your future operational processes. If these resources still have responsibilities within the organization while trying to do their job on your digital transformation program, your chances of success are significantly hampered."

"Are those all the business process team roles?" Mike asked.

"Not quite. You've also got business process subject matter experts (SMEs)—individuals who have a peripheral relationship to the program. They are the individuals who remain with the business to handle the day-to-day operations of the business while the digital transformation program team defines the new way to do business.

"They are, however, a very important part of the process. These individuals are brought into design workshops for their specialized knowledge on the key processes they know within the organization, as well as what I call their 'tribal knowledge' for how things really work. They are also brought in for process reviews, conference room pilots, and testing throughout the program so they will start getting a feeling of what their new world will look like prior to being officially trained on the new solution. These are also going to be the future 'hearts and minds' you will be transforming as you are re-envisioning the new way of doing business, so you want to keep them engaged, at least at a peripheral, at what you are doing by showing the prototypes and demos of what the future processes, technologies, and data will look like as you are developing it.

"Then you've got consultants," Jonas added. "Business process consultants (system integrator/independents)—these are specialists who know your industry very well, know your industry process area very well, and know how to use the core technology to be used as part of your digital transformation to make your business process work within your industry. These are the guys that you will come to rely on to help guide you through the challenging road ahead in defining what your future-state organization will look like and how your business processes will operate within your environment."

Mike saw how the various groups of the business process team worked, but he knew it would still take a while to help define how all the resources would be used. "And that's just the first category!" he exclaimed.

Jonas smiled and nodded back, taking another drink. "It's all in that prep kit[2] I gave you, which I jokingly call 'If Jonas were King,'" Jonas said with a big grin. "In all seriousness, the prep kit I gave you sort of lays out my philosophies on how I do this type of work based on a lifetime of experiences solving these types of problems. It should come in handy from time-to-time.

"Next comes technology teams. Although digital transformation initiatives are chartered to re-envision new ways to do business and solve those business problems, there are a lot of technology-related components needed to make it all work. So, when setting up the technology area of your digital transformation organization, you will need to consider your technical organization for these areas. If you are using a packaged software application as part of your transformation (likes Salesforce.com and SAP), you are going to have a configuration team with expertise in the software package as well as one or many of the business processes that are within the scope of your program. You will also have multiple development teams depending on what they are developing. For example, custom coding within the package (for functionality you need that does not exist within the package). Business analytics that are a combination of report writers, data scientist, and dashboard developers that help take complicated information and present it in a way to help your leadership make more informed decisions. Then you have your infrastructure team, which is responsible for all of the hardware, networks, and performance of the software. Then you have the security/governance, risk, and compliance group, which is responsible for protecting your software and data and building the appropriate controls so that resources cannot abuse the processes and procedures while keeping your leadership out of jail."

"Jail?" Mike blurted.

"Yes. Don't worry about it, though. But before we get too carried away, I want to mention **enterprise architects**—those individuals within your current organization who know the current technical architecture of your legacy appli-

----

2 Please visit **www.platinumpmo.com/thetransformationbook** to access the prep kit.

cation environment and are heavily relied upon for working with your digital transformation technical architects to ensure you have a solid future state-integrated architecture. Lastly, legacy application teams—these people are a really important part of your digital transformation implementation as you will be working with them a lot when it comes to interfaces and conversions and system retirement strategies. Engage with them early and make sure they know what your future architected solution will look like. Their insights, along with your enterprise architects, will be invaluable."

"And if you consult with them too late, you may not understand the entire image of what we want the company to be after the transformation is implemented," Mike added. "So data teams would be next if I remember correctly."

Jonas smiled. "Right on both counts. So, there are a couple of data team options you should consider: Each process team can have its own data part, or the data team can be its own organization."

Mike asked, "Is one better than the other?"

"Well, 'better' might not be the right word," Jonas said carefully, "but I prefer that the data team be its own entity with its own staff that works hand-in-hand with its process counterparts. If set up properly, your data management team under your data organization can and should be treated like a process team because data management is just as important as order to cash or record to report from an organizational process perspective. But that's not all there is to say about data teams. You need to look at data from a perspective of data migration as well as on-going data governance."

"Data migration teams are primarily focused on the one-time event of getting information out of our legacy environments and into our digital transformation solution environment, right?" Mike asked.

"Yes. There's a *tremendous* amount of effort that goes into extracting the millions and millions of records out of dozens if not hundreds of legacy application environments, transforming that data so it meets the rigorous standards necessary to operate in your new environment, and then properly loading that information into your new environment."

Mike whistled. "Sounds like a tall order."

Jonas was getting excited. "Now, to properly perform these actions, you are going to need folks who really know their data as well as the business pro-cesses that use that data. But at the same time, you are going to want to put some processes in place to ensure that once you convert that data and it is all cleaned, transformed, and ready-to-go in your new environment. You want that data to stay clean and continue ready-for-use in your environment. That requires what is called data governance, and the types of folks who will help you with this really know their data as well as the business processes that use that data. With me so far?"

Mike gestured for Jonas to go on. "So, this group starts off in a dilemma: How do both data migration work and data governance work at the same time? This can even be further complicated depending on the service providers that your organization has contracted to do the work. I've have been on clients where they had one vendor responsible for the processes and configuration of the application, three different vendors responsible for the extract, transformation, and load aspects of the data migration, and yet another vendor responsible for establishing and developing the master data governance. That is really compli-cated stuff!"

"That's a lot of vendors!" Mike said, understanding what Jonas was getting at.

"The other complication I have traditionally run into is that the organiza-tion doesn't really have many people that *really* understand how the data is used within the organization. So, the internal selection pool to staff this part of your digital transformation organization is often limited. But I have some good news: A lot of the work that is done to get your organization ready for data migration is a significant subset of the same work that is needed to establish the cleansing and transformation rules for data governance. You may want to consider com-bining your data migration and data governance into one team. Now, this does have some risks, but after some thorough risk analysis, it may still be your best course of action."

Mike thought for a moment. "I'll get back to you when we have a decision."

"Excellent," Jonas responded. "So then, the last component I wanted to mention is organizational transformation. Depending on your structure, you can have three or four different teams under one umbrella: The communications team is responsible for processes and coordination of program-related internal and external communications. The training team is responsible for creating the program's end-user training, which could take on several forms, including traditional classroom training, webcast training, and some newer adult techniques called 'microlearning' through knowledge as a service (KAAS) solutions. One service that comes to mind is a company called Ringorang.[3] Ringorang is an incredible platform that allows you to take the key concepts taught throughout your traditional classroom and webcast end-user training and positively reinforce the key transformative learning through gamification. It is really a neat concept.

"The organizational transformation team is responsible for preparing the organization for fundamental changes that will be taking place as a result of your digital transformation such as organizational structures, process changes, and knowledge transfer. The transformational benefits team—which I have seen as either a sub-team under the OCM track or as a program track all on its own—is responsible for granularizing the benefits identified during the business case, identifying 'owners' within the organization who will sign up to be accountable for delivering those benefits, and then working with those leaders to help them transform their organizations.

"Now, these transformation activities are usually integrated with the OCM activities and are designed to not only support the new business processes and technologies but to put these leaders in the best position to achieve the benefits for which the program was chartered and to which they are being held accountable."

The two just sat in silence for a moment. Jonas finished his water, and Mike looked off into space, processing what Jonas had told him. It was all in Jonas' prep kit, which he had read—mostly—but to hear this man explain it all from memory was impressive. And a little intimidating. Once again, Mike was struck by the fact that he was fishing in deep waters. However, he also had a guide who really knew his stuff.

"I hope I answered some of your questions," Jonas offered, looking at his watch.

"We have a lot to think about," Mike agreed, "but I see why you organize teams like this."

---

3 For more information on this tool, please visit www.ringorang.com

"I know we didn't talk a lot about the program leadership and governance[4] side, but it's in your prep document, so I thought I'd spare you my speech on that for the moment," Jonas said with a grin.

"Small favors," Mike replied with a laugh.

Jonas got up, tossing his empty plastic bottle into the recycling bin. "We can work more on this later. I know you've been with the organization for some time and know a lot of the key personnel. You'll probably have recommendations for people you'd like to have on the program. You'll want to work with their bosses to try to secure their services, and it will be a tough sell because the bosses don't want to lose these resources because they depend on them for the day-to-day operations. This is where the decision board, steering committee, sponsor, and CIO come in to help influence the decision to get the right people for the program—it's the company's future.[4]

"If you'll spend the time to front-end load the organizational structure of your teams," Jonas said as he headed for the door, "you'll reap many rewards later."

"The influence of the decision board, the sponsor, and the CIO will be the key helpers in making this happen and will help navigate the politics. And I have a clear directive," Mike said as he walked Jonas out. "Thank you again—the info you sent is really useful, but when we go over it like this, it really comes together."

Jonas gave him a single, affirming nod. "My pleasure, Mike. See you tomorrow?"

"Bright and early."

* * *

Mike spent the next few weeks carefully selecting his project leaders and trying to thread his way through the minefield of how the program would ask for qualified people to step out of their existing positions to help the initiative for the company. He knew he'd get pushback because no one wanted to lose their top people. But he knew that if he didn't get some of Extron's best into the program, his task would only be harder.

----

4 For more information on the program leadership and governance side and other topics, as well as the prep kit, please go to **www.platinumpmo.com/thetransformationbook.**

Despite his volatility, Mike did end up selecting Chet Osborn; the potential upside was just too great for him to ignore. However, Mike was mindful that "potential" was a compliment when one was younger, and the older a person got, the less of a compliment it became. However, he hoped that Chet's full potential could still be realized and that he would be able to harness the man's best for the duration of the transformation.

Chet would lead the integration team. He knew the legacy environments like few others, and he understood integrations. Mike was counting on Chet to bring a lot of technical brilliance to the program and that he would be able to handle the other man's potentially less-developed skills, like communication.

Chet's reputation was for being very smart but not the best with people. His intelligence and work ethic had brought him up quickly, but as he had to handle more and more leadership responsibilities, his rise had faltered due to his abrupt, abrasive personality and poor leadership style. Mike, however, was hopeful that a new opportunity would give Chet his chance to learn from his mistakes and get his career going again.

"I guess we'll find out," Mike said to himself.

Mike had known of Gina Paterno since he started with Extron. She had been around for a few years before he got there, but while Gina was competent and seemed to like her job, she'd never seemed too interested in advancing her career. Her performance reviews seemed to reveal a woman who was afraid to take risks and chose to play it safe. She was consistent, dependable, and deferential.

Mike quickly became convinced that Gina's trouble wasn't vision—it was confidence. He'd tapped Gina to play a pivotal role in the data team, leading the data subject matter experts through the migration and governance aspects of data. She'd been an end-user in customer service for most of her career, and she knew Extron's systems inside and out. Gina had also been in the supply chain area of the corporate office for the last few years, so she understood supply chain and manufacturing extremely well. Her role would help ensure that Extron's customers had a positive experience after the transformation. She'd never been part of a major project, but since she had so much tribal knowledge, Mike thought she'd be a great asset to the program.

He was also hoping that this role would be a steppingstone for what he wanted her to do toward the end of the program, running the operational readiness team. Because Gina came from the business and would learn along the way what program and project life were like, Mike was thinking that she would be a great asset in helping the program prepare for the digital transformation cutover that was eventually going to come down the road. When he sat down to talk with her about it, however, her lack of confidence was pretty evident.

"But I've never been on a project before," she said hesitantly when Mike explained the situation.

"Well, this is a 'program,'" Mike corrected gently.

"Ok," Gina replied. "I don't know how to execute at a program level. I've never done this before."

"I understand," Mike told her. "I've never been a program manager before, either." He smiled at her. "But I've seen your work. I think with a little help, your tribal knowledge could really be of value in leading our data SMEs through the data migration and governance work. Then when the time is right, and we both agree it would be a good fit, I would like to consider transitioning you to leading the organization through our cutover."

"And you want *me* to do this job?" she asked.

Mike nodded. "Gina, you do great work. And I'm going to help you. Personally. I honestly think you simply need a boost to your confidence in yourself. Anyone who knows our business operations, data, and people as well as you do is going to be a real asset to this team. You just need do what you're good at. I'll help you with the rest—if you're willing."

"You're really offering me this job?" she asked reluctantly.

Mike laughed a little, good-naturedly. "Yes, I really am!"

"And you'll help me?"

"I will," Mike replied.

Gina considered for a moment and then said, "Can I think about it?"

Mike smiled. "Definitely."

She thought about it for two days, and then Mike began a new journey as a leader by starting to mentor Gina. He made it his point to build her confidence, and over the weeks that followed, he began to see a transformation coming over the shy, competent woman.

Mike met with Gina regularly over the ensuing weeks. She was good at her job, no doubt about that, but she was hesitant and unsure of herself. She would defer or bog down on decisions, and Mike guessed that she was probably a high "S"—steadiness—on the DISC personality profile, with some "conscientiousness" thrown in for good measure. A week later, he was proved right when they did the DISC personality profiles as a leadership team-building exercise, and Mike's understanding of what she needed to make decisions grew. He started listening to her differently, and his coaching evolved to fit his new understanding of her personality, motivators, and strengths.

His leadership team was coming together.

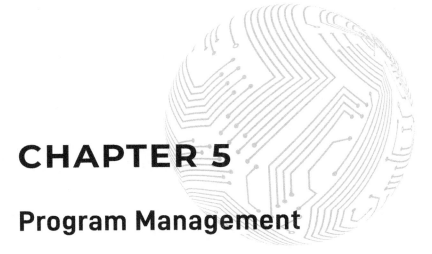

CHAPTER 5

Program Management

"**J**onas, is there anything you're not an expert at?" Mike joked as they left together from a session with the key members of the leadership team on the initial draft of the overall benefits case for this initiative. "You've got a real handle on project management, too."

Jonas smiled back as they walked down the hall. "I'm terrible at poker and landscaping," the older man replied.

"One of the things I have been really struggling with to get right in my head is how to structure the overall program plan for this initiative. It's a pretty massive amount of work that is going to require dozens of teams, hundreds of resources, and tens of thousands of hours of work to deliver; and somehow, all these efforts need to work together in some coordinated fashion so that, at the end of the day, the whole enterprise will work in a new digital model. So, my question to you is, how does one go about structuring a behemoth initiative like this?"

"Well, that is why I am around here to help you, Mike. It's all about setting up your program management for a successful outcome. Have I ever told you where I got my inspiration for project management?"

Mike shook his head.

"Two historically significant individuals: The Iron Lady, Margaret Thatcher, former prime minister of the United Kingdom—she said, 'plan the work...work the plan.'" Jonas ticked one of two fingers off his left hand before going on, "and another great man who said, 'a plan is really good until you get punched in the mouth.'"

Mike felt himself grinning fiercely. "Mike Tyson!" he said, recognizing the quote from the former heavyweight champion of the world.

"From those two modern-day 'philosophers,'" Jonas continued, his eyes twinkling, "I've created my own digital transformation project management quote: 'Plan the work and work the plan, but be prepared to get punched in the mouth along the way.'"

Mike laughed as the two reached his office. "Is that what just happened in there?"

"A little bit," Jonas chuckled. "What you saw in that meeting was your leadership coming to grips with the potential value of this digital transformation could mean to Extron and their future. They are looking five-to-ten years out into the future and imagining the possibilities. It's pretty important stuff. At the same time, they are seeing how they are being positioned to be on the hook to deliver these potential benefits once the initial transformation is complete so there is a little hesitation in their commitment.

"Based on what I have seen in the past, there is going to be quite a bit of conversation and negotiation among the executive leadership to pin down the big 'value buckets' that they see will meet their strategic objectives and getting the right executives to sponsor and deliver those benefits once the transformation starts to become operational. Once these decisions are made, it will really go a long way in helping you understand what your scope is going to be and how your program is going to deliver it."

"So, what do I need to learn about program management, oh wise one?" Mike asked, half-joking.

"Well, I think we should discuss some approaches and some of the leading practices I have used to structure your plans to provide you the ultimate flexibility and allow for you, as a program manager, to get consistent measurement across all of your projects within your digital transformation program."

"Sounds good," Mike replied. "So how *do* we go about organizing our digital transformation program plan? Because I'm pretty sure what we just saw isn't it."

Jonas nodded and took a seat in Mike's office as they entered it. "That's a tough question. Ask ten different people, and you will probably get ten different answers. Each one of those approaches has its own unique pros and cons."

Mike grunted. "That's not the answer I want; I want you to just tell me what's best and save me a lot of frustration and man-hours."

"At the end of the day, you want an approach that will work best a program of your size and will provide you the most flexibility in measuring all of the integration points across the myriad of projects within your program," Jonas answered.

"So, one size *doesn't* fit all?"

"Exactly. All have pros and cons, but you want to look at which approaches offer the most flexibility—decentralizing or integrating."

"Okay," Mike said as he got them each a bottle of water. "So, how do we know which will work best for us?"

"Let's look at it from a 50,000-foot view," Jonas suggested. "That far out, most organizations are structured similarly, like this." He took out a piece of paper and drew a pyramid on it with four levels. He began scribbling in names, with "company" written at the top. "You will have a 'company view.' A company can have several organizational decompositions. Depending on those decompositions, a company can have one or many portfolios of initiatives where they are trying to achieve maximum value for that line of business within the organization. Portfolios could be owned by a variety of sponsors, but for our discussion today, let's assume that the portfolio level is owned by your organization's CIO, Charles Offerman. With me so far?"

Mike nodded.

Jonas went on, "The portfolio view is where you will house all of the initiatives, or programs, that your organization desires to accomplish. The challenge is there are usually many more programs that an organization wants to execute than the organization has resources or the finances to accomplish. This is where portfolio management comes into play. Within portfolio management, your portfolio manager, Charles, will work with the executive stakeholders to determine which desired programs provide the most strategic value to the organization, have the resources and capital support to execute the program, as well as an appropriate risk profile that indicates a high probability successful completion.

"A program is classically defined as a group of projects coordinated to obtain benefits not available from managing those projects individually. In other words, for your larger digital transformation program, you will have a variety of different projects to coordinate under the umbrella of your digital transformation program."

"All right," Mike agreed. "So, if we're defining terms, what's a 'project' to you?"

"A project is classically defined as a temporary endeavor undertaken to create a unique product, service, or result. A project is traditionally where you associate a commercial (or legal) statement of work. I say this is the traditional place where you manage your SoW."

"My pig? I don't have a pig," Mike teased.

"Your statement of work," Jonas clarified, grinning back. "It really depends on your engagement with external partners at the program level. If your program is being delivered by all internal resources, or if you have one and only one external partner to support you on your digital transformation program, then you could have your SoW at the program level. However, most of the larger digital transformation initiatives, like yours, that I have experienced have multiple external partners—each with their own specialization that is needed to achieve the results of your digital transformation. Therefore, it is better that you structure your SoWs at the project level."

"So, I need to organize all my pigs at the project level," Mike said, trying to make it funny through repetition. Jonas just smiled and plowed ahead.

"To define your statements of work, you need to define your scope for each of your statements of work (or if you are doing it at the program level, the statement of work for the entire program). One of the best ways to start building the scope of your program and the future projects within your program is to look at your scope from a variety of levers, which, when combined, will give you a pretty good picture of the scope of your end solution."

"What are the levers?" Mike asked.

"Think of them as segments or considerations when defining scope. You want to look at scope from a variety of viewpoints (i.e., levers) to make sure you have a holistic picture of everything you have to do. For example, here are the levers I usually consider when trying to define a program or project's scope:

"Software—what software applications are going to be the foundation for your digital transformation, or if you are developing from scratch, what development platforms are you going to be using? You guys selected SAP for the supply chain and asset management process areas and Salesforce.com for the marketing and customer relationship process areas, so we can mark those down.

"Next comes organization—what parts of your organization are in scope for this digital transformation? Is it isolated to one or many business units? Is it isolated by a set of plants or facilities? Is it isolated to a geographic region? Or is it the entire global enterprise? What jobs are going to be impacted as a result of this program? These types of questions help drive significant portions of your organizational transformation scope.

"Then comes the business process—what business processes are being digitally transformed? This goes back to our conversations around value streams in our planning session. Think of all the different value streams that are in scope for this digital transformation program. For example, market-to-opportunity, opportunity-to-cash, plan-to-produce, procure-to-pay, record-to-report, hire-to-retire just to name a few.

"Okay, next we have reports, forms, and analytics—what reports and forms will need to be developed for this implementation? Which data analytics platform will be used (this should also be defined as part of your software scope), and exactly what do you intend to develop on that data analytics platform?"

"Well, as you said, Jonas, one of the packages we've selected is SAP, and from what I have learned about SAP over the years, it already comes with thousands of pre-defined reports and forms."

"Yes, yes it does," Jonas replied. "However, what you will find (and what your end-users will find most of the time) is that those reports are pretty generic and some to most of the time, they miss the mark of what your transformation will need in terms of operational and strategic reporting. By all means, you will be able to leverage those built-in reports; however, from my experience with other clients, they will need to be modified to meet your needs.

"This is all part of defining the initial scope for your reporting, form, and data analytics. What you are trying to do with this lever is establish a high level framework of the estimated number of reports, forms, dashboards, and data analytic views you think will be needed to (1) operate the business and comply with all financial and statutory requirements, (2) measure the benefits from your business case, and (3) provide the analytics to leadership to help them make strategic decisions. Does this make sense to you?"

"Yes, it does," Mike replied. "However, I have no idea just how many of these we are going to need."

"That's okay, Mike. I recommend using a little 'statistical guessing' to size the initial scope of this lever. This is where you are going to rely on the experiences of your chosen solution integrator, or integrators, to get their assessment and guidance and then build that into your initial scope for approval. Then, as you go through the design of the transformation, these numbers will get adjusted through your scope management processes—another topic for a future conversation."

Jonas continued, "Then we have interfaces and integrations. What interfaces are you going to have to develop to integrate this new digital transformation technology to the remainder of your future state operating model? How are you going to develop those interfaces? Point-to-point or through an integration engine? If it's an integration engine (again, this should also be defined as part of your software scope), what and how do you intend to develop on that integration engine?

"Conversions and migrations—are you going to be getting rid of current solutions as part of this digital transformation? How are you going to convert that data? What tools are you going to use to convert that data? Is your data old and out of shape? I think you might need to consider a rigorous data cleansing initiative because there is no sense in putting bad data into a new digital transformation product. Once the data is in and clean, how are you going to keep it clean? What about General Data Protection Regulation (GDPR)? What tools will you need to govern your data moving forward? The outcomes of these conversations will drive your data migration scope and help further define your software scope.

"Enhancements and workflows—take into consideration the foundational software packages selected, and the high-level list of requirements developed from your digital use cases. Will your selected software package cover all of your requirements, or are you going to have to build additional enhancements to that software or build custom workflows to help with the automations in your new digital solution?"

"You know, I've been wondering about that," Mike confessed. "I've thought we might need to build some custom workflows that we just haven't talked about yet."

"Well, now's the time," Jonas told him.

"So, what's next? Or is that all?"

"Not quite. You also have security and job roles—what security is your new digital solution going to need? How are you going to protect your company's digital assets? Your user's privacy? What job roles are going to be impacted by this security model? What compensating controls are you going to have to put in place? These definitions drive a major component of your organization's transformation.

"Then we've got infrastructure—what hardware and network infrastructure will be needed to run this new digital solution? And finally, mobility—what mobile devices are going to be supported by this new digital solution? How will they connect? What custom development will be required to allow your users to function while they're mobile?"

"Overload!" Mike complained. "I've read your stuff on this, but all those questions—it's just so much. How do we answer them?"

"One at a time," Jonas answered soothingly. "All of these things are elements of defining exactly what is and is not in scope for your program. By thinking through the levers of scope, you should have a pretty good idea of what is in and what is *not* in scope for your digital transformation initiative. This is a really important moment because this scope definition will be the basis for your future planning. It will help define what program roles you will need to deliver this scope, what estimating factors you need (or need to develop) to determine the standard efforts for the work packages required to deliver this scope, and how many resources you are going to need by role within your program organization to meet the timelines you set out to deliver this initiative. All of this information drives into your program's statement of work."

Mike nodded slowly. "That statement of work has been hanging over me for a while now," he admitted.

"Let's go grab some lunch," Jonas suggested. "I can go over some of the methodologies if you'd like. That may help."

"That sounds good," Mike agreed. "Let's hit Angela's. I could use a good sandwich."

The two grabbed their stuff and met up a few minutes later in the parking lot. Jonas rode with Mike, which was his standard procedure. He waited until they'd ordered and sat down before he went on, though.

"After you define your projects under your program and your high-level scope of each of your projects, you need to determine which methodology each project is going to execute within your program. Here is where it can get a little tricky and where the relationships with your external partners really come into play. For example, your core process and functional configuration teams may want to follow an agile approach where you define chunks of the functionality and deliver results in sprints of work.

"Your data migration team may want to follow a hybrid approach, what I like to call a 'watergile' approach, where you spend a lot of time upfront looking at the complete design in a more traditional waterfall methodology approach. However, once the initial development is completed, you then go into an agile sprint methodology where you are driving final data results in sprints of time.

"Then you have your organizational change management methodologies that use an entirely difference nomenclature. For example, the ADKAR methodology developed by Prosci, which stands for awareness, desire, knowledge, ability, and reinforcement."

"Are those totally different than waterfall and agile?" Mike asked.

Jonas wagged his hand back and forth. "Sort of. Just by the name alone, you would have a hard time understanding where the actual components of this methodology would fit into a traditional waterfall or agile-based methodology. But they do have certain things in common, and their principles can be applied in either a waterfall, agile, or watergile approach."

"So, is everyone just going to be using their own methodology? How will I keep track of that or make sense of it?"

Jonas answered, "There are a few ways as the program leader that you can handle this. If you like a completely integrated methodology for your program, then you need to work with your external partners to redesign the phases, activities, and tasks of their individual methodologies into the chosen methodology structure of your digital transformation program."

"So, get them all onto our page?"

"Right. However, If you are comfortable with a decentralized approach, then allow each of your projects to use their methodology of choice and use the other metrics within your program, which I'm about to show you, plus program-level milestone indicators to maintain congruence across all of your different projects."

"That sounds pretty complicated."

"My philosophy is to allow your external partners to use the methods they use to be successful; that is one of the reasons why you hired them. As a program leadership team, you can put in the structures and flexible pivot points into your governance model to allow each project to run using their methods. However, integrate the key metric points between their methodologies and your program governance model to maintain congruence across your entire program."

"So, you're saying to do whatever approach works best for them to position them to succeed?" Mike confirmed.

"Correct. You're hiring them for a reason—they're supposed to be good at what they do. So, let them do it," Jonas said before continuing. "You know, Mike, you are asking some really great questions, and I know that sometimes I am giving you the traditional consultant's response of 'it depends,' which can be frustrating. But in this case, it really does depend on hundreds of factors you need to consider while coming up with a structure you think it is going to work. The good news is that you are not making these decisions in a vacuum. You are going to get the opinions of your solution integrators, you will have my thoughts, and you will also be able to bounce your ideas of your boss, Charles, to get his feedback. You will get to the right answer. Just remember to lay out a flexible program framework that will allow you to pivot just in case you get punched in the mouth."

I have to be Mike Tyson, Mike thought. *Better get my boxing gloves.*

CHAPTER 6

Program Plan Structure

Jonas and Mike were still at lunch at Angela's, enjoying the place's famous sandwiches while Jonas continued helping Mike understand program planning and tracking. Mike was plowing through his New York Special—pastrami and deli mustard on rye bread—while Jonas was barely making progress on his own turkey bacon ranch.

"Once you have defined your projects and methodology approach, you can start building out your program plan structure," Jonas said before eating a handful of chips.

Mike asked, "How do we start?"

"You do this by building a work breakdown structure or WBS—which is, as you might guess, a structured way to break down your work. As I have mentioned, there are a lot of ways to create a work breakdown structure. I have tried dozens of different approaches over the years, but I'm only going to give you the two I like best: integrated and decentralized."

Mike said, "You mentioned those two before. How do we know which we want?"

"At the end of the day, it will be up to your comfort level to decide which approach works best for your digital transformation program. However, once you see the details of each approach, you will see there are common elements or 'metadata' that exist between the two approaches, which should give you comfort that if you choose one approach and are not comfortable with how it is going, you could pivot to the other approach and still maintain your program integrity."

"I like that," Mike said, and then he took a big bite of his sandwich.

"Let's start with the example of an integrated program plan," Jonas said. "Level one: If we are using an integrated program plan approach, we have most likely decided to use an integrated program methodology. Therefore, the first level of our work breakdown structure would represent the different phases within the chosen methodology for your transformation.

"Level two: Define major projects, project teams and/or project elements within the program. When we've talked before, we have defined our level two to represent our projects as our process teams and enabling workstreams (process, technology, data, and organization transformation)."

"Right," Mike said, remembering.

Jonas went on, "Level three: Regardless of your thoughts on the structure of level one and level two—because this is what will change if it's integrated or decentralized—level three is where the rubber starts meeting the road. What is it that you want to deliver in your digital transformation? Therefore, level three represents the types of physical deliverables you are going deliver within that phase of the program within that project team. At level three, there is a loose correlation to what you defined as part of your levers of scope. For example, you defined things such as interfaces, conversions, reports, enhancements, etc. Well, at level three, you could define deliverable types such as interfaces, conversions, reports, enhancements, and so forth as well. This helps provide a logical correlation between your scope and your work breakdown structure. It doesn't have to be one for one, but it will help connect the dots between your scope and what you intend to deliver.

"Level four traditionally represents the actual deliverables, which tie to the deliverable types you defined at level three that you are going to deliver within the scope of that project team. Level five represents the actual work packages one has to produce to complete a deliverable. Let me give you an example:

"To complete an enhancement deliverable at level four, there may be three separate work packages that need to be completed first, such as:

1. the enhancement functional specification,

2. the enhancement technical specification, and

3. the enhancement code and unit test results.

"You can see how we started at the highest level within our program, and within five steps, we were able to get to the most granular task we can accomplish on our program. Pretty cool, right?"

Mike nodded, taking another bite. He'd seen this on Jonas' "If Jonas Were King" document and his "Developing an Integrated Program Planning & Governance Framework" document, but hearing him go through it helped put the pieces together. "What about decentralized?"[5]

"Then we just flip levels one and two. What this allows the program to do is segment each project into a unique project plan using its own methodology. We can still get granular in just five steps."

"But there's not like a 'right' and 'wrong' work breakdown structure?" Mike asked.

Jonas shook his head. "There are different ideas for selecting the right WBS for you. As I mentioned before, you may or may not like these approaches for your own structure and may want to come up with your own way. At the end of the day, there isn't one 'right way' to do this. What I have found through the years is that if you are capturing these key metadata elements, you can have absolute freedom in structuring things just about any way you want."

"So, what is the metadata that we need?" Mike asked.

"Within your project plan, you are going to set up metadata that represents these key fields: Your *'Program ID,'* your *'Project ID,'* your *'Methodology Phase ID,'* your *'Organizational ID'* (represented as a value stream or enabling stream), the *'Deliverable Type ID,'* the *'Deliverable ID,'* the *'Work Package Type ID,'* and the *'Work Package ID.'*

----

5 Please visit **www.platinumpmo.com/thetransformationbook** to access the prep kit.

"Next, for each line item that you have in your project plan, you must assign a value to each of these metadata elements. Once you have done this, you have a variety of ways to slice and dice information with your plan, and as long as all of your projects within your program are capturing these fundamental data points within their projects, you can maintain integrated congruence within these projects."

Estimating the WBS Through Work Packages

Mike said, "Well, if I am understanding everything you have said, Jonas, through this approach, we can build pretty detailed project plans down to the work package level that tell us everything we need to design and build for each deliverable, how those deliverables roll up to each project, as well as how those projects roll up to our overall program, correct?"

"You are correct, sir," Jonas said, smiling in his best Ed McMahon impersonation.

"So, now that we have all this information, how long is it going to take to complete the work?" Mike asked.

"Well, it's a matter of estimating the effort of your work packages. Once we have established all of the deliverables and work packages for our projects within our programs, we need to shift our thinking to how we are actually going to build those work packages and the time and effort it will take to do so. For each type of deliverable that you are going to deliver, you should identify the standard work package types that need to be completed to complete that type of deliverable. Let's continue to use the example enhancement delivery type we were talking about a few minutes ago. In our example enhancement delivery type, there are three enhancement work package types: a functional spec work package, a technical spec work package, and a code and unit test results work package.

"Now, enhancements can be very simple or very complex, so we need to establish estimating ranges for these levels of complexity. Now, this can get a little complicated for a variety of reasons, including methodology and the external partners being used to complete a deliverable type, which I can explain later.

But in its simplest form, you are going to build a standard low, medium, high, and very high complexity estimate for each of your work package types within your deliverable types that you can provide to management as a standard 'rough order of magnitude' estimate at the deliverable type level."

"So, we're just guessing."

"Well, it's educated guessing. This is where your solution integrator partner, or partners, come into play because they have been there and done this before. Based on their history of similar types of programs and projects, they should be providing you with these kinds of insights and rough order of magnitude estimates. These are the kind of questions you want to ask in your request for proposal. This way, you will be able to get a variety of responses from different vendors and use the estimates they provide in their RFPs to come up with a blended estimate for each of your standard work package types that you can then roll up into a respective estimate for each deliverable type.

"Now, bear in mind that the estimations you get in the RFP may be a little on the low side. The reason is that these vendors are all trying to win your business; therefore, they are going to propose the most cost-effective solutions with the general assumption that your implementation is going to go perfectly. Then they will have a risk and assumptions section that will point out things that 'might' go wrong, but they won't put that into the price because they want to be as close to—if not the—lowest-cost bid. This is where having an independent advisor comes in handy to help you navigate these situations and help you come up with that blended estimating model that you can use independently to share with your leadership what you think it will take versus the bids received by your potential partners."

That RACI Thing

"That is some great insight, Jonas—thank you," Mike said. "Based on what you've told me so far, we've used the levers of scope to define our high-level scope, and we have built work breakdown structure down to the work package level. Now we can put some estimates around what it's going to take to complete each of those work packages, correct?"

"You are correct again, sir!"

"So, I guess my next question is, who's going to do the work?" Mike asked.

"Ah, good question," Jonas said. "Remember when we first met, we were talking about how to set up your organization?"

"Yeah."

"Well, in that conversation, I described all the different roles large-scale transformation programs like this one need to be successful. What we are going to do next is take those roles we defined and start assigning them in what I refer to as the integrated RACI."

"Yeah, I remember talking about that RACI thing."

Jonas continued, "So, RACI is an acronym that stands for responsible, accountable, consulted, and informed. And to address your question, in my experience, the way most digital transformation programs use RACI charts today offers very little value in helping programs or projects with daily operations. You see, most organizations use RACI charts to identify which organizations are responsible, accountable, consulted, and informed at the statement of work milestone or deliverable level. This is great for understanding the commercial responsibilities, but what problem does that leave?"

"It doesn't help you get the job done."

"You got it," Jonas affirmed. "So, as part of my way of handling digital transformation program planning, I want to get some true value out of these RACI charts, so I re-envisioned how they could be used."

"Oh? Do tell."

"As part of my re-envisioned approach, I define our RACI profile at the work package level. Therefore, for every work package within our scope and plans, we will define who is responsible, accountable, and needs to be consulted and informed for that work package. In short, this approach will provide you great value in program estimating, program tracking, deliverable and work package management, communications management, risk management, issue management, key decision management, formal change request management, and those changes that happen during a program that fall under the radar."

"So, pretty much everything that has to do with actually getting things done," Mike observed before finishing his sandwich.

"Do you want me to go more into the various resources in RACI?"

"Yeah, please," Mike answered, fishing deep into his chip bag for the last holdouts. Jonas hadn't made as much progress on his own meal—too much talking.

"The responsible resource works on the work package, delivers the work package, brings the accountable and consulted resources into the decision-making process to help complete the work package, schedules the sessions necessary to get clarity around the work package, provides solution recommendations based on subject matter expertise, gets the necessary sign-offs from accountable and consulted resources, and provides updates to accountable, consulted, and informed parties. As part of our leading practices, I recommend that you appoint one and only one responsible resource per work package."

Mike nodded. "Okay. That makes sense."

"The accountable resource for a work package has ultimate accountability for the work package," Jonas said as he held up fingers and began ticking them off as he went through a mental list. "He or she assigns or provides recommendation on the responsible resource. If consensus is not derived, he or she makes the final decision on how to move forward, removes obstacles blocking the responsible from being successful, ensures responsible has all the tools to successfully accomplish work package, may champion change requests that are driven from the work package level, monitors responsible progress, and provided updates from responsible. Again, you only want one accountable resource.

"The consulted resources for a work package provide industry or business expertise in defining or clarifying requirements for the work package, traditionally sign off on the results of the work package, are available to the responsible party as needed, and are provided updates to progress on status of work package from responsible party.

"Lastly, the informed resources for a work package receive status on the work package and receive information on key risks and issues impacting the ability to deliver the work package against critical path items."

"You can have a lot of those last two types of resources," Mike observed.

"They're the people in the trenches getting things done."

"So, we can hope," Mike added wryly.

Jonas took a big bite and chewed before going on. "Want me to really rock your world?"

"Rock away," Mike said with false bravado.

"Okay—now, depending on your point of view and methodology bias, this could be a little controversial. The classical definition of methodology as it relates to program and project management is defined as a strict combination of logically related practices, methods, and processes that determine how best to plan, develop, control, and deliver a project throughout the continuous implementation process until successful completion and termination. With me?"

"Definitely. Sounds pretty standard."

"So, I want you to focus on the phrase 'logically related.' As you have defined your work packages, there is a logical relationship among those work packages that tell the logical sequence in which the work packages can be performed and the logical handoffs between these work packages. Now, this is pretty cut and dry with methodologies that follow a more traditional waterfall approach to completion. However, the lines tend to get a little blurry when you start using more agile-related approaches to your development methodology.

"In a traditional waterfall approach, you first build your functional requirements, get it signed off, then build your technical specifications, get them signed off, then do your development and get that signed off. This makes for a very cut and dry series of dependencies amongst these three work packages, right?"

Mike nodded but didn't say anything.

Jonas went on, "However, in an agile approach, you traditionally sign off on the final functional requirements much later in the game after you have already done some technical design and some development as part of the iterative sprint executions. Where it can get a little cloudy is in the formal signoff.

"Regardless of your methodology biases, the facts remain the same. For all intents and purposes, there are relationships among all of the work packages defined for a given deliverable. Your job here, Mike, is to *understand* those relationships and build the interdependencies among those work packages so you know *which* sequence to execute the work. Now, mind you, this does not mean that each work package within your deliverable needs to be performed in a serial fashion. On the contrary, there are many work packages (based on their interrelationships) that can be performed in parallel."

"That would definitely save time. I wouldn't risk having some resources waiting around."

"You're getting it. One of the techniques I use that increases the probability of completing deliverables on time, reduces the risks of missing requirements, increases the understanding of functionality, and reduces general miscommunications is to have continuity amongst the key resources throughout the lifecycle of a deliverable. We can accomplish this by using that integrated RACI approach I just told you about.

"When building out our RACI chart for each of the work packages associated with a given deliverable, we want to keep continuity among the key personnel throughout the lifecycle of that deliverable. This is where the agile methodology works great because of the product team's focus built into how these types of projects are organized. For waterfall type projects, maintaining this type of resource continuity can sometimes be challenging.

"Let's say we have a functional consultant who is responsible for completing the functional specification. A functional manager is his or her accountable, and the functional consultant will also have a planned technical designer as well as business subject matter experts as the consulted parties to help build out all of the functional requirements for this enhancement. As a courtesy, the functional consultant will keep the technical manager informed on the progress and results of the functional specifications work package.

"So, let's talk about the consulted assignments for a minute. By having both the business SME and technical designer engaged as the consulted parties, you accomplish several objectives: first, you increase the probability of fulfilling the needed requirements to successfully develop the enhancement deliverable. Second, you engage the technical designer early in the process, which increases the understanding of the requirements, reduces the risks of misalignment or miscommunication on the requirements, gets initial insights on the technical implications surrounding the requested requirements, and increases the throughput of the future technical design. That means you start building a cohesive set of 'teams'—or if you are in the agile world—'tribes' of resources with multiple disciplines who are working towards a common goal of completing a deliverable. Is your world rocking a little yet?"

"So, you can use RACI to help make sure we're completing deliverables on time and help prevent missed requirements?"

"Exactly," Jonas said. He took a really big bite, smiling around it as he chewed and watched Mike try to process everything he'd just said.

CHAPTER 7

The Chain Factory

Mike was now done eating, and Jonas had nearly finished his meal. Mike's head was still full of what Jonas had been telling him about project management.

"So, assigning the roles we defined into the integrated RACI helps us define who will do the work," Mike said. "And now that we have all this wonderful information captured, you can put it into a project plan, and it will tell us everything we need to know and give us the perfect answer, right?"

"I wish it were that easy. Most of the time, this is where our problems begin, and it's because of how we structure the plan and circumvent the functionality of our planning tools to achieve a given date. You've probably heard people say that if they just work really hard, they can hit overly aggressive dates. Well, I can show you some techniques that I have learned that will put you in a position to achieve even those unrealistic program dates set by management *without* killing most of your team in the process."

"That definitely sounds good," Mike quipped. "Dead team members aren't usually too happy. So, what's this trick?"

"First, I want you to think of your digital transformation program like a big factory, and you, the program lead, are the plant superintendent. As the 'super,' you are making widgets, and to make those widgets, your raw materials need to go through a variety of work centers to get fabricated, and your workforce is the folks who run those work centers and fabricate the product until it comes out the end of the manufacturing process as a brand new shiny widget. So, if your digital transformation program is the factory, think of your work packages as widgets, your teams as work centers, and your team roles as manufacturer labor."

"Do I get to wear a hard hat?"

"If it makes you happy. Don't interrupt—this is good. Sometimes, a work center can't keep up with the flow of production that the preceding work center is providing, right? This causes wasted capacity in the next work center, which causes wasted production in the entire operation. What can we discern from this?"

Mike grinned. "So, I can talk now? Okay—maybe that a product can only be produced as fast as the slowest part in the process?"

"I'm tipping my invisible hard hat to you," Jonas replied. "Okay, Mr. Super, what would you do about that?"

"I would find a way to somehow improve the throughput of that one work center so that it is running faster."

"How fast?" Jonas asked.

Mike thought for a moment. "As fast as the others?"

"Okay," Jonas said, moving on. "Assuming we can get it to go as fast and be as efficient as the others, what then?"

"Do that as many times as necessary until they're all balanced and working at the same speed?"

"Excellent, young disciple. There's hope for you as a factory super. You want the right balance of speed, throughput, cost, and quality for the stuff your 'factory' is producing. Only your digital transformation program is your factory, your work packages are your widgets, your teams are the work centers that can bottleneck, and your team roles are manufacturer labor."

Critical Chain Project Management

Jonas went on, "Similar to the manufacturing process description, your digital transformation program can be filled with bottlenecks and wasted capacity that can impact your ability to deliver on time and within budget. And wasted capacity can literally cost you millions of dollars."

"Which we do not want," Mike added dryly.

"No, we don't. We have hundreds—if not thousands—of work packages flowing through our different project teams, project roles, and team members, and most of them are integrated in some way, shape, or form. Because of the inter-dependencies of these work packages and the relationships that they have to other project roles and project teams, very little time is given to see what bottlenecks are happening in our digital transformation program supply Chain. Therefore, we need to take a look at how we can best identify, analyze, and (hopefully) remove these bottlenecks in our program supply chain.

"Which brings me to the program management technique I most want to talk to you about. It's called critical chain project management. Most project professionals have heard the term 'critical path' and have a pretty good idea what that is."

Mike nodded. "I remember discussing it when we first met, but just in passing. I get the feeling you're going to fix that shortcoming in my project management education."

"A program's critical path is the longest connected path of activities (or work packages in our case) that need to be completed to complete the program. The critical path technique was developed in the 1950s and is still used today. And it works great in certain conditions. You may know of a famous program in the 1960s that used the critical path technique."

"I do, actually," Mike said triumphantly. "It was what helped NASA and its Apollo program to put a man on the moon."

"Gold star for you. Now, what is the one thing that NASA had in the 1960s that most programs today do not have?"

Mike thought for a few moments, but Jonas answered for him. "A near-infinite supply of money! We were in a space race with Russia at the time, and we needed to be first to the moon."

"I know I work for a utility," Mike said, "but we still have to justify our spending. So, let's assume that I can't just print money."

"So, for all the rest of us program leaders who are held to something called the triple constraint, it's a constant juggling act between three factors: scope, time, and cost. So, how can we do the best possible job of predicting our critical path in correlation to our triple constraint? *The critical chain approach.* What the critical chain approach does is not only build the critical path of your program based on the structural dependencies you define from start to finish; it also takes into account the resources available to perform that work on those structural dependencies."

Mike interjected, "I've used tools like Microsoft Project's resource leveling, and they did an okay job of leveling the plan based on resource constraints."

"There are more powerful tools out there that have more evolved algorithms and do a better job of showing you the resource bottlenecks within your program," Jonas responded before continuing. "So, let's put all of these pieces of the puzzle together on how to build a successfully integrated digital transformation implementation plan:

▶ **STEP 1** – define your scope.

▶ **STEP 2** – build out your anticipated teams to support the scope of your digital transformation *and* define the different roles you will need within each of these teams.

▶ **STEP 3** – build out your work breakdown structure by determining

  ▶ your different projects,

  ▶ your different methodologies,

  ▶ the deliverables within the scope of each of your projects,

  ▶ the work packages needed to complete each deliverable,

  ▶ the estimated level of efforts to build each work package, and

▶ the interdependencies amongst the work packages within each deliverable.

▶ **STEP 4** – determine the roles of who will be responsible, accountable, consulted, and informed for each work package.

▶ **STEP 5** – build an initial plan to establish the critical path for each project (and, therefore, your entire program).

▶ **STEP 6** – use the critical chain planning technique to identify role level bottlenecks and identify ways to remove those bottlenecks and reduce the time to deliver your program."

"Okay," Mike said. "That's pretty logical."

Jonas replied, "By performing these six steps at the role level, you will have a good idea of just how many resources you will need and the skills they will need to possess to deliver your program. However, the work doesn't stop there. Once you start staffing your program and projects, you go through the same exercise, but this time using real resource names instead of roles and start balancing out those resources so that you derive a resource-based critical chain that aligns closely with your role-based critical chain."

Tracking Your Program

Jonas was done eating, but Mike could tell the discussion wasn't over.

"Now," Jonas began, "let's switch gears a little bit. Now that we have 'planned the work' and built this incredible digital transformation implementation plan, it's time to work the plan and start protecting yourself from getting punched in the mouth. As I mentioned when we started, I recommend three ways of tracking the progress on your digital transformation implementation journey. The first one is your traditional quantitative measurement approach. Using our factory analogy from before, you can also think of it as: 'How many widgets did you plan to build for me today and how many widgets did you actually build for me today?'"

"So, we're verifying that we're getting it done."

Jonas nodded and continued, "Based on the project plans you produced using your project planning tool, your tool has derived the estimated dates in which you are forecasting each and every work package to be completed. If you were to take these work packages and associated dates and plop them on the trend line, you should get a line that looks something like an 'S.' You might have heard of this as an 'S-curve' chart (or if you are an agile person, a burn-down chart)."

Mike had heard of that. "So, the general rule of thumb is the closer your lines match—or the further my line representing the actual cumulative number of work packages delivered is above what we planned—the better your project or program is running, right?"

"Well, so goes the traditional thinking," Jonas replied slowly, taking a drink of his soda. "This is an approach that many consulting companies, external partners, and agile practitioners use today to measure just how successful their projects or programs are running. When I see this as the primary way of measuring success on a digital transformation program, I get a lot of heartburn because I know it's just a matter of time before this program gets punched in the mouth. The program is getting played like Muhammed Ali's rope-a-dope, and it is just a matter of time before you get that uppercut and—*bam*! Your program is out on the canvas."

He had said that so suddenly that Mike actually jerked back a little. Other patrons looked over to see why the older guy was yelling at the younger one, but Jonas didn't seem to notice.

"I can show you the statistics and mathematics as to why looking at this measurement as the only lens is a bad idea," Jonas said, "but there is one thing that I need to bring up to you that I have seen happen on a lot of programs over the years: optical manipulation."

"What do you mean?" Mike asked. The shock of the moment had passed, and he was once again entirely focused.

"Not all work packages are created equally, correct? Each has their own unique level of complexity. What I have seen in past programs are external partners working on the easier 'low hanging fruit' work packages and getting those done—but circumventing the work packages that are on the critical path or critical chain, just to show a positive trend on their S-curve report. This is not something that is in the best interest of the program, but it is a tactic I have seen used time and time again to keep problems within the program under the radar of the program management team."

"Okay, I hear what you're saying," Mike replied. "So, what do I do instead? How do I deal with this?"

"These are a couple of reasons why I am not a big fan of this measurement technique as a sole source of information," Jonas replied. "So, here's what I recommend: The critical chain fever chart is a measurement tool that I really like. It does, however, require that you use the critical chain planning and execution technique for it to be of value. With this approach, we are not necessarily looking at 'planned vs. actual' work packages that have been built; we're looking at how much of the critical chain of the program has been completed vs. the amount of buffer you have allowed for that program."

"Buffer?" Mike asked.

"I don't want to go into too much detail right now, but think of the buffer as a collective amount of time we are going to put at the back end of our project plan to account for all the unplanned 'stuff' that happens during a digital transformation implementation.

"Imagine a chart[6]," Jonas said. He grabbed a napkin and pen and started drawing. "The horizontal axis represents the percentage of the critical chain completed, and the vertical axis represents the percentage of program buffer used. There is a secondary vertical axis that is used to predict when the critical chain will be completed.

"I like to use red, yellow, and green areas on the chart. As you measure progress using your critical chain project planning and execution tool, the software I use is determining what percentage of the critical chain is completed and how much of the program buffer has been used. This is plotted at each measuring point, and depending on which color your plot point lands on, it gives you a really good indication of the health of your project or program.

"If your plot points land in the green zone, you are in good shape. If your plot point lands in the yellow zone, you should be cautious and start investigating what is going on that is causing the increase in buffer usage vs. completion of your critical chain. And if your plot point lands in the red zone, that is a good

---

6 "Please visit **www.platinumpmo.com/thetransformationbook** to access the prep kit."

indication that your plan is not working, and you need to do some serious work to get the train back on the tracks. This is usually an indicator that critical resources are being over-utilized on activities that are not on the critical chain and that your accountable resources need to do a better job of protecting those resources."

"So," Mike said, taking mental notes, "stay out of the red. Got it. So, what was the third technique you mentioned?"

"It's one that I learned early in my career, and I have been using for years. While the first two techniques are more objectively and statistically driven, this technique provides a very subjective assessment of your program by looking at seven key areas to each digital transformation's success:

1. We need to measure that stakeholders are committed.

▶ Are the stakeholders known and available?

▶ Are their interests and influence identified and managed?

▶ Are the stakeholders pleased with the progress of the digital transformation and the work being delivered?

▶ Is the program managing their change over time?

▶ Are stakeholders available to the program?

"This technique will require deliverables and work packages generated by the organizational change management team to help assess how well the program's stakeholders are performing.

2. We need to ensure business benefits are realized.

▶ Is the value proposition on target?

▶ Can optimal solutions be identified?

▶ Does the program sponsor have confidence in the project's delivery?

▶ Can the delivery organization measure and highlight specific results?

"This technique requires defined deliverables and work packages as part of the benefits realization team and project to measure the benefits realization effectiveness of the program.

3. We need to check to see if work and schedule are predictable.

▶ Is the program plan as well as the individual project plan up to standard?

▶ Are the milestones met and critical chain on track?

▶ Is the work proceeding in line with the plan?

▶ Is the program sponsor updated on the status of the work?

▶ Are actuals vs. budget being tracked?

"This can be measured by the work packages established and managed by your program management office. You will be taking some of the objective and statistical program results to provide a subjective measurement and analysis of the work and schedule.

4. Verify that scope is realistic and managed.

▶ Is scope clearly and mutually understood?

▶ Are the individual statements of work understood by all partners and agreed upon?

▶ Are only the deliverables within scope (no more—no less) being executed?

"This can also be measured using the program's change control process, current scope vs. original statements of work to assess just how well scope is being managed.

5. Check whether the team is high performing.

▶ Does the team have the required competency and capacity?

▶ Is there a consistent dialogue between PM and team?

▶ Are adequate facilities in place?

▶ Is the team working normal working hours?

▶ Is the team working efficiently?

▶ Is personal development happening and in line with expectations?

▶ Are key resources staying with the program?

"This technique has some objective measurements if you analyze the critical chain and resource capacity management reports provided by program planning software. As for the other components, it will require observation and interviews to develop an assessment."

6. Observe if risks are mitigated.

▶ Are the teams aware of potential risks and documenting them in the risk register?

▶ Are the teams notifying their project managers when work progress is threatened?

▶ Are actions being taken to reduce or eliminate risk?

▶ Are risk management processes established and followed?

"This can be evaluated by the analysis of the effectiveness of your risk management process and the risk exposure your program has actually incurred or realized during the lifetime of the program.

7. Realize the benefits of external partners.

▶ Are the external partners' delivery organization stakeholders known?

▶ Is internal knowledge from the external partners being harvested and leveraged for your program? Are the external partners harvesting knowledge from this digital transformation to improve their toolset?

▶ Are actuals aligned within budget?

▶ Are the external partners in line to receive favorable project citations from your digital transformation effort?

"This measure is often overlooked. If your program is a true partnership with your external partners, then you want your program to be a win-win relationship with your external partners. Making sure they are successful is just as important as your success."

"So, you let the stats drive the first two techniques, but this one is a more subjective assessment. I can see why you need them together," Mike commented.

Three Different Lenses

"Using all three together has helped me many times," Jonas began. "In one of my digital transformations, I was able to use all three measuring techniques to provide me a comprehensive picture of what was going on at this point in this particular program. As part of one of the program standard reporting periods, we generated the results of the S-curve report. When looking at the reporting period from an S-curve perspective, we were looking pretty good. We had lost a little of our gain over the past couple of weeks, but we were still tracking ahead of our overall work package build plan. However, when I looked at our critical chain report for the same reporting period, I got the proverbial 'punch in the mouth.'

"In looking at our fever chart, we had gone completely in the red and had consumed all of our buffer for the reporting period. Well, as you can imagine, I was kind of shocked at seeing this and immediately went into tactical mode to find out just what was going on."

"What was wrong?" Mike asked.

Jonas grunted. "When getting into the details of the remaining critical chain, I notice a severe bottleneck in one of our critical resources, and his work packages and his remaining estimated ability to get those work packages completed was what was pulling the entire program behind."

"So, one guy had put you into the red?"

"This led me to perform some subjective analysis on the state of the program. In reviewing the project plans, timesheets, and through conversations with key resources, we were quickly able to determine the problems. Certain resources were working extraordinary hours while other resources were under-utilized. We were able to reallocate qualified resources who were—at that moment under-utilized—to take on some of that work and regain a majority of our precious project buffer and get the program back on track."

"But if you had only looked at one of those tracking reports, you could have gotten an entirely different perspective. That would've been bad."

"It could have put the whole program in jeopardy. So, please, to maintain a fair and balanced perspective of your program, look at metrics from a variety of different lenses, and don't be afraid to ask questions when you see outliers from some of those results."

"I feel like I learned more about program management at lunch today than I have in the last few years," Mike said as they gathered up their trash and headed for the door.

"I've gotten punched a few times," Jonas said. "Early on, you don't know what's happening or what to do about it. Your precious plan falls apart, and suddenly you're over time and over budget. Entire transformation initiatives can be at risk."

Mike held the door open for Jonas. "So, it's great to have a plan and work the plan—thank you, Ms. Thatcher—but without some Mike Tyson in there, you're not going to know how to respond when you have a problem."

"And you *will* have a problem," Jonas said. "It's just a matter of when."

Mike shook his head a little and laughed dryly. "Thanks for the positive outlook, Little Miss Sunshine."

"Thank me later, Mike," Jonas said. "You'll be glad you know this stuff when you get hit."

CHAPTER 8

Problems

Mike was thinking of what Mike Tyson had said about getting punched in the mouth as he drove home. All this information on project management—and how tenuous and volatile it all seemed—had him feeling insecure again. He wasn't sure he'd be able to juggle three different types of reports effectively to keep his finger on the pulse of the transformation, but knowing that he didn't have to do it alone set his mind at ease.

As Mike was pulling down the street to his home, he started to make the mental switch from "Work Mike" to "Family Mike" and prepared to hear about the day from his wife and kids.

Blending broken families is never easy, but there was something about his connection with Nancy that he'd never had in his first marriage, and it carried them through the difficulties. He and his ex had gotten some counseling along the line and learned some tools, which had taught Mike he needed to be emotionally available and vulnerable with Nancy if he wanted to build trust and intimacy. One of the habits that helped keep them close was that Mike made a habit of sharing his concerns and misgivings with her—even when he wouldn't tell another living soul. She did the same. Then, they always sat together and figured out one thing they could do, together, to address the problem, even if that just meant talking again the next day.

With Gabbi, who was only fourteen, encountering drugs so young, the family dynamics became more disrupted. It looked like they'd have a whole new set of challenges to tackle together.

As he pulled into the garage, Mike thought of how Nancy had patiently endured so much with him as his career developed. She'd supported him as he put in the long hours just so they could make it. She'd encouraged him when he got his lumps, celebrated his wins, like the Workseam Project, and talked him down from the ledge of anxiety when he realized how much was riding on the success of that job. Through it all, she'd been an amazing mother while her own career path slowed to a crawl.

With the pay bump he'd gotten with his new position, Mike wanted to hire someone to start cleaning their house, and he wanted to put the kids in this good private school they'd always wished they could afford. He figured that together those things may help free Nancy up so she could give her career some more attention—if she wanted to.

Mike walked into the house to find the lights off. Nancy's car was in the garage, so he had expected to find her with dinner going and music on like usual. Instead, everything was quiet and dark.

Putting his work bag and jacket down, Mike walked through the house with a growing sense of unease. What was going on?

He finally found her sitting quietly and staring through the windows that overlooked their back yard. She held a tissue, and he could tell she'd been crying, but she was quiet now. His own thoughts forgotten, Mike eased down next to her and quietly asked, "Nancy?"

It took her a moment to respond. She turned slowly, eyes haunted. "They want to do a biopsy."

"What? What happened?"

It took her a while to respond. "I went in for my normal screening—and they saw something. A lump."

Mike was speechless. Nancy was only thirty-eight, way too young to be dealing with this. Breast cancer was something older women got, wasn't it?

After a moment, she went on. "So, they said that women my age have denser breast tissue, so they weren't sure at first. I guess the last time it just looked like fibrous tissue, but now..." She was quiet for a moment. "Now they want to check it—a biopsy."

"When?" Mike managed to get out, his throat as dry as a desert.

"Next Monday," Nancy replied. "Can you take me?" As she said it, her reserve crumbled, and the tears came rushing back. She reached toward him, and he scooted closer, taking her in his arms.

"Of course," he assured her. "We're in this together."

CHAPTER 9

The Budget Planning Meeting

Mike pulled his car into an open parking space at work, and once again, he realized he'd spaced out on the drive—but this time, it wasn't because he was thinking of the digital transformation. His excitement over his new position and new responsibility had been lost in the vortex of Nancy's news, which was terrifying.

The doctors weren't messing around with this lump. Nancy was only thirty-eight, and they were going to move aggressively to find out what it was and begin treatment if necessary. Nancy was scared; she had family members who had fought breast cancer, and she knew something about what that road looked like.

In the wake of Nancy's news, Mike's confidence in his ability to tackle the transformation had crumbled. How would he be there for her if he were the director of this massive undertaking?

Feeling like a man facing a firing squad, he forcefully shoved the car into park, grabbed his stuff, and headed inside for a budget planning and cost management meeting.

He'd just been punched in the mouth. How would he respond?

The Meeting

Despite how much Mike and Jonas had been talking about this meeting, he wasn't looking forward to it at all. Jonas could talk about negotiating win-win deals all he wanted to; the reality was that Mike was the one who had to get down into the weeds and try to pull out a good deal for the company. He just had to find a way to deliver everything on time and at (or under) budget, which required the right arrangement with the consultants.

He tried to remember everything he and Jonas had prepped for: Take the data from their initial planning efforts and use that information to start the budgeting process. Then extend that work to fill out the individual human resource budgets and expenses, plus any non-resource related expenses associated with the program. At which point, they'll try to negotiate a "win-win" deal while looking at what those look like from an Extron's perspective and the consulting companies' perspectives.

Jonas felt that Mike needed to be able to see the situation through two lenses—that of his company and then also the consultants' lens. "That's the only way you'll be able to architect something that is a win-win," he'd said. Extron's perspective hinged on the overall cost of the digital transformation. Mike knew that he had to work with these people for the foreseeable future, and if their margins were not up to snuff, they could provide less experienced and cheaper resources to make up the difference, which would put Extron's transformation at risk.

According to Jonas, a critical key to success was the realization of their internal benefits, as well as his own companies' benefits.

So, Mike knew he'd have to work together with the consultants to ensure that Extron's interests and theirs aligned.

In preparing for this budget meeting, Mike spent dozens of hours going over the three proposals of the firms that were invited to partake in the oral presentations for the work. All three firms presented highly compelling cases as to why their firms should be selected to be the partner of choice for this initiative.

Mike remembered sitting down with Jonas after the final oral presentation and having an informal debrief. One point stuck in Mike's head, and he couldn't shake it. He'd asked Mike if he had noticed just how poised each pre-sentation team was and how, as they were presenting their estimated timelines and resource plans, just how simple and confident each were—as if this trans-formation was going to be a walk in the park.

Mike could recall a similar feeling that Jonas had described. Then Mike remembered the look that Jonas gave him at that moment. He'd stared at Mike with intense eyes and said, "Don't get bamboozled here. This transformation is far from a walk in the park."

Jonas went on to tell Mike about their positioning: "Similar to when you first start dating someone, you are always trying to be at your best and trying to impress your date. In the case of these vendors, they are trying to do the same thing. Each wants to marry you (get the contract) and is trying to persuade you to the altar by showing you how easy it is going to be and that you will live happily ever after if you just marry them. When in reality, this transformation, like a mar-riage, is going to be tough. Things are not always going to go according to plan, you will fight and disagree, your plans will change, dates will be pushed, and costs will most likely go up."

Jonas counseled Mike to review the three proposals and build his own hybrid model using the three proposals—plus the lessons that Jonas taught him about critical chain budgeting. And that was what Mike did on a Tuesday night after his family had gone to sleep—try to come up with how to realistically tell his leadership what he thought it was *really* going to take to deliver this trans-formation.

On Wednesday morning, Mike entered the meeting room and set up his laptop. Melissa Kotel, from finance and the budget specialist, was already there—she was always early—and Mike could see Jeffrey Allen, head of supply chain, headed down the hall for the meeting room. He walked in a moment later, followed by Marilyn Kelliher, head of customer relations.

Mike greeted everyone and then asked some light personal questions as they got settled—nothing too invasive but enough to show he cared. He was glad no one asked about Nancy; he wasn't sure how he'd respond.

In the previous meeting, Jonas had provided an executive overview of some of his key budget-making principles that he had used with his other clients, including a high-level overview surrounding the principles of critical chain program management and risk planning and how they can be used to build more realistic planning budgets.

Mike got down to business by saying, "I'd like to start this meeting by quickly going over the three proposals that are being considered and compare them to some of the work I did this past week using the concepts that Jonas shared with us in our last meeting."

Mike spent the next thirty minutes going through how he took a hybrid of the three proposals and built out a high-level critical-chain composite plan and budget model of what the program could look like in terms of time and expense.

They could all see what the critical chain for a perfectly executed plan looked like, assuming they wouldn't use any buffer.[7] But thanks to Jonas, not only did they know this was unrealistic, they knew they could reasonably project more realistic numbers.

"For our estimating purposes," Mike began, "I am assuming that ours and our partner's day-to-day management team will be working through the entire buffer consumption—not just the 'project completion date' according to the project plan. Remember, we intentionally leave these roles out of the critical chain planning and focus on the roles that are doing the work to maximize the most exploited resources on the chain, which are usually day-to-day operations resources."

Mike explained that they would need to add their overhead roles that need to be part of their budget, such as project managers, program directors, etc. "In these roles, you may forecast part-time equivalency hours." Jonas had told him that depending on the size of the program and management oversight needs, these roles may be planned at less than forty hours per week. "But, again, we need to tread carefully here; we don't want our project management team to become a bottleneck in our ability to deliver this program."

"I think we need to consider something else," Marilyn said. "The reality of a forty-hour workweek. There are a lot of factors that go into this, depending on your lens. If your resource roles are in-house and are salaried resources, then planning forty-hour workweeks should not be a problem."

---

7 Please visit www.platinumpmo.com/thetransformationbook to access the prep kit and to learn more about critical chain project planning.

Mike understood where she was going and stepped in as she paused. "But if our resource roles are consultants or hourly employees, then we need to look at this with a little more granularity, right?"

"We are capturing the estimated rate per hour each resource role is going to cost the program," Jeffrey pipped up. "If you are looking at this from a consulting organization perspective, those roles that they are supplying to this program become the estimated billing that they will be charging for their consulting services. Therefore, hours above forty would be charged as well."

Mike nodded. "Good point, Jeffrey. This is a risk point for us. We will need to factor over-time policies into our commercial arrangement language as well as possibly some 'not-to-exceed' clauses.

"Let's shift gears into the next section of the budget—expenses. Our resource roles can be broken down into two primary categories: non-travelers and travelers," Mike said.

"Non-traveler resources typically have very little expense overhead—usually 0-5 percent of their billable value. Non-traveler resources typically fall into three buckets:

1. Those resource roles that you are staffing in-house within your organization.

2. Those consulting resources that work either off site or off shore, and you will be working with remotely.

3. Those consulting resources you hire in your local market who will commute to your place of work on their own dime.

"The other category was traveling resources. These resources have to commute long distances, which traditionally requires airfare, lodging, car rental, meals, etc. Estimates vary on a case-by-case basis, but usually, expenses for these types of resources range between 15-25 percent of their billable rate. As part of our RFP, we provided each vendor with our corporate travel expense policy and asked if they would follow it, and they all agreed.

"As part of the budget modeling I have done, I assumed that all 'on-site' consultants will have an 18 percent travel expense, and all of the 'off-site' consultants will have a 4 percent travel expense to account for the possibility of them taking one or two trips to our office. I assumed that all of our employees will have a 1 percent travel expense for off-site meetings and other events."

Sensing the travel conversation was over, Melissa quickly segued into another area of budget concern. "We need to consider the non-human costs of the program as well." She began ticking items off on her fingers as she went through them, "Okay, so:

▶ Do we have hardware to lease or purchase?

▶ Software or cloud services to purchase?

▶ Are there going to be internal cost allocations to consider for organization administrative overhead?

▶ Is the program going to have to pay for additional staff augmentation to backfill for resources taken from the organization to work on your program?

▶ What about office space, additional furniture, equipment?

▶ Are there going to be flat-fee travel expenses in your future not covered by our resource expense plan?

▶ Is there any additional training that our program team will need to go through to successfully execute the digital transformation initiative?

▶ Do we need to consider any retention bonuses or any other employee incentives for the extra work they will be performing on this program?

▶ Are you planning any program related outings or staff recognition events?"

"Excellent points, Melissa. Excellent indeed. I have taken a first-pass at those estimates on page twelve of the deck," Mike said, impressed with her understanding of the issues. "As you can see already, the figures we are coming up with here are considerably different than the figures provided to us by our three vendor proposals. I don't know about you, but I don't want to be the one to paint an unrealistic picture of what it's financially going to take to deliver this initiative to our leadership, but at the same time I don't want to sandbag the numbers, either. I want to provide our leadership with a statistically driven set of figures that we can all support and that we can realistically deliver when it is all said and done."

Win-Win—Or No Deal

Next, Mike teed up the next topic they'd have to prepare for. "Okay, we will soon be making a decision on which vendor to select. I want to start the negotiation processes with all three vendors to start aligning terms and conditions before making our final decision, as this is a significant weighting factor in our overall vendor selection scoring model.

"There is a very famous book that I am sure most of you have read, or at least heard of, called *The 7 Habits of Highly Effective People* written by the late Stephen Covey. If you have not read it, I highly recommend doing so.

"Habit four centers around some core negotiation scenarios that are available to us in any type of situation and one that sticks out as the best scenario of all." Mike began to lay out the various options that he and Jonas had talked about earlier:

"Scenario one: We win, they lose. The win-lose scenario seems to be the one we're told to aim for. Relationships between clients and vendors, managers and employees, and competing suppliers are designed as a competition, with each party investing in their personal outcome at the expense of another. Us winning means them losing.

"In a negotiation," Mike went on, "the supplier tries to get the price as high as possible while the client tries to get the price as low as possible. Managers apply systems, structure, and pressure to get the most productivity out of staff while employees attempt to work as little as possible for the highest wage. Organizations strive for monopolies by attempting to hurt their competitors. But I don't think this is a viable long-term strategy because we're going to be working with this primary vendor for years."

Heads around the room nodded in slow understanding. Mike went on, "Scenario two: We lose, they win. The competitive environment aimed at success for your type-A personalities can drive other temperaments toward a lose-win scenario. In lose-win, one party continually feels the need to capitulate to the other. Similar to abusive relationships between individuals, both parties develop a common understanding of the power imbalance. Not going to happen.

"Scenario three: We both lose."

Jonas had said that he had seen a lose-lose scenario when everything fell apart. Both parties decided that neither can win. All efforts were spent ensuring the other party loses as badly if not worse than the other. Jonas had explained that digital transformations solved complex business needs, and the opportunities for conflictions between scope, schedule, and budget were significant. Often, when projects did not meet expectations, the relationship quickly soured. In the worst situations, Jonas had said that other vendors or system integrators have picked up the pieces of a program from other suppliers. In these programs, both the client and the previous supplier had been more intent on causing as much pain to the other party as possible than they were on resolving the issues.

"But here's the one we want," Mike told the group. "Scenario four: We win, **and** they win—**or** no deal. Either we both get an acceptable outcome, or the deal is off—*and that's okay*. Each party agrees that the project, contract, and even the relationship may terminate if the parameters are not acceptable."

Jonas had explained that this was an incredibly liberating perspective to have when going into negotiations. "If the nature of the sale is not going to meet the client's objectives and be sustainable for the company, you need to be prepared to walk away," he'd said. "From the client's perspective, if my services cannot align with what the client is after, then there may be another company more suited for the work."

Mike instructed, "As part of our negotiations, always seek to have a 'win-win or no deal' frame of mind."

This took them a moment to grasp. They'd all been operating under the assumption that the goal was to get a win for the company, even at the expense of another. Mike knew it wasn't malicious; it was just seen as good business. What he was telling them went against that unstated imperative.

Jeffrey said, "It's a good perspective to have Mike, and we should all work towards this goal. They are going to be our partners—hopefully for a long time. We will do our best to negotiate a win-win deal and provide our recommendations on our selection to the executive steering committee."

Agreement Structure

Jonas had prepared Mike for the meeting by telling him that when working with large-scale (typically multi-year) digital transformation initiatives, you traditionally established a three-tiered agreement structure.

"At the top is your master services agreement," Jonas had said. "This describes your long-term business-to-business relationship between the organization and the consulting organization. Here you define your enterprise-wide terms and conditions and agree upon a global rate card for all future engagements over a given time frame.

"The next tier down is referred to as your master statement of work. This traditionally ties back to the digital transformation initiative and the program scope that the consulting organization has in relationship to the overall digital transformation. From an organization perspective, you may have one or many master statements of work associated with your digital transformation initiative based on the different vendor partner relationships you have engaged in your digital transformation initiative.

"Within these master statements of work with your individual providers, you lay out the governance roles and responsibilities, the financial structure for the program, and overall master program framework (even though you may be only providing a portion of the work to any given service provider).

"The final tier is the individual statement of work. This provides the specific scope of work in relation to the overall program. In our vernacular, think of this as an individual project within a program. This is the actual financial commitment your organization is giving to your consulting partners for a specific scope of work."

Jonas had finished by saying, "By providing the third tier in this structure, you are giving some flexibility to the long-term outlook of your digital transformation initiative. We all wish we had a crystal ball and could predict the perfect outcome of our digital transformation future effort, but things happen. There are business down-cycles, unforeseen acquisitions, and vendors who fail to perform as once intended. By releasing individual statements of work over time, you have the flexibility to pivot should any of these (or any other) conditions arise."

Mike relayed all this to the individuals in the meeting to explain why he wanted individual statements of work to come out over time and keep them flexible. As he explained, he watched their heads nod in understanding.

CHAPTER 10

Contract Financial Structures

M ike, Melissa, Jeffrey, and Marilyn were still knee-deep in their budget planning meeting, and with each topic they covered, Mike became more and more glad that Jonas had prepped him so well. They'd discussed the three common financial structures together, which he hadn't gone into in detail during the meeting: time and materials, fixed bid, and hybrid risk/reward. Each had its own pros and cons.

Jonas had briefed him: "With a time and materials financial structure, your organization pays for each and every approved hour billed by the consulting organization, plus all approved expenses submitted by the consulting organization. This type of arrangement, in a pure form, typically favors the consulting organization because they are paid for every hour of service produced regardless of value outcome."

Mike hadn't liked that if there was not a strong partnership in place with a win-win mindset, the program could be at risk, as they may think the consulting organizations did not have a lot of incentive to finish on time and within budget which could lead to budget control issues down the road.

"What can we do about that?" he'd asked Jonas.

"With a fixed-bid structure," Jonas had explained, "the organization and consulting organization agree on a fixed price to complete a specific scope of work. This type of arrangement does have some win-win tendencies but typically favors the organization. From a consulting organization perspective, this could be a fairly profitable arrangement, assuming a few conditions are met.

"From an organization's point of view, there are also some pros and cons," Jonas had gone on. "The biggest pro is that you know upfront what the cost is going to be, and it is up to your partners to deliver the agreed-upon scope for that cost. The potential downside is going to be a very active change control process because your consulting partner (if managing their scope correctly) will be pushing everything that was not defined as part of the scope through the change request process for further compensation. Again, depending on the strength of your partnership, this could get adversarial over time if not properly managed."

Jonas had saved the best for last, and this was the one Mike pitched: "A really good 'win-win' model is a hybrid risk/reward model that has components of the time and material *and* fixed bid models. This model demonstrates a fair allocation of risk with meaningful incentives to hold each party accountable for its performance based on roles, responsibilities, and expertise and provides a financial structure that ensures that the consulting organization's incentives and interests remain aligned with their partner's interest."

Win-win, Mike had thought.

Risk and Reward

Mike explained to the attendees that he wanted this fair allocation of risks and incentives for their arrangements with their contractors. After listening to him recount the information Jonas had shared with him, everyone seemed to agree that this was reasonable.

"What I really want," Mike then began explaining, "is to make sure we don't get caught in a trap of pouring more and more money into this because we didn't budget effectively."

"We could use a not-to-exceed cap," Melissa ventured.

Mike and Jonas had actually talked about this, but he wanted to hear it from Melissa.

"The budget performance strategy with a not-to-exceed cap can be defined as a time and materials project with a not-to-exceed cap based on the percentage of the project budget baseline. If we had a million-dollar project with a not-to-exceed cap of 110 percent, that means the highest out-of-pocket cost for time and materials would be 1.1 million dollars.

"You can also apply the same type of logic to expenses and put incentive and risk structures around those as well," Melissa went on. "For example, with a not-to-exceed cap of 18 percent for expenses, the maximum expense exposure we'd have is $180K, making your total program fee exposure for this consulting organization 1.28 million dollars."

"I like where you're going with this," Mike affirmed. "Let's quantify our budget performance risk/reward a little further. From a consulting organization's perspective, there is a risk that the program will go over budget. If it does, a percentage of the resource rate would be deducted based on a rate reduction scale.

"For example, in our million-dollar program scenario, if the actual program fees were greater than $1,050,000 but less than $1,100,000, then there would be a resource rate reduction of 50 percent. If the program were to go over 1.1 million dollars in fees, the resource rate reduction would be 100 percent and the consulting organization would be working for free until the statement of work was completed.[8]

"On the flip side, there is the reward. If the consulting organization uses less than 95 percent of the budget, they will get 50 percent of the difference as a budget performance bonus. If they use 95-100 percent of the budget, they will get a 25 percent bonus of the difference."

"That really makes it in their best interests to stay in the budget, then," Jeffrey admitted.

"What about the scheduled performance?" Marilyn asked.

"Okay," Mike said, glad she'd asked. "Now let's explore the schedule performance side a little further. With a schedule performance risk/reward struc-

---

8 For more information, please visit **www.platinumpmo.com/thetransformationbook**

ture, a percentage of each invoice is held back from payment in the event of any problems in delivery schedule performance for a given milestone or project."

Marilyn asked, "Are vendors going to agree to that?"

Mike shrugged. "From my conversations with Jonas, it's a pretty common practice for transformations like this. Let's say we're using a standard invoicing schedule. However, 10 percent of each invoice is held back as part of the schedule performance plan, which is tied to specific milestones within the program. If the milestone is completed one week ahead of schedule, then the consulting company gets rewarded with a fixed-fee bonus. If they finish two weeks ahead, then it's an even bigger bonus. However, if they are late by a week, then 50 percent of the holdback amount associated with that milestone is forfeited. If they are more than two weeks late, then the entire holdback amount is forfeited."

"That's both a lot of reward and a lot of consequence. Do vendors really go for this?" Marilyn asked.

Mike nodded. "As I understand. The big players are used to this, and they see it as a way of getting a win for their company; they're going to see this an opportunity to increase their profit margins through prompt delivery."

"Won't they just pad their timeline?" Jeffrey grumbled. "You know, say it will take longer than it really will?"

Mike thought for a moment. "Well, they are all still competing for our work at this time. I think we should apply this as part of our negotiation. If one of our vendors balks at the notion, it's deducted from their overall vendor selection score. If all three balk, then we might have hit a nerve and may want to reconsider it. Conversely, if we see changes to timelines and budgets as a result of this point, then we can have a better feel for the challenge this may bring to our partner and act accordingly. That being said, I doubt this is the first time any of these have heard of this type of request from one of its customers, so I think we should be in good shape."

Quality Performance

"So, that takes care of the timeline component," Melissa said, thinking out loud, "but how do we know if they'll do a *good* job or if they'll rush it to get their reward?"

"That's a really good question," Mike agreed. "I asked it while I was learning this stuff. Quality performance is a measure that's a little harder to quantify but is associated with budget and schedule performance. As part of quality performance, there must be client approval on all deliverables (whose completions drives back to the budget and schedule performance metrics). However, this is not an open door for the organization to intentionally delay signoffs to avoid paying bonuses. Remember, we are talking about win-win partnerships here. We can offer them a time limit on the number of days we have to approve the deliverable. If not approved by then, the deliverable is automatically approved.

"The second component is the quality reviews of the consulting organization. This is usually completed by a QA partner within the consulting organization and can either be built into the cost of the service or treated as an additional cost.

"A third component is an independent quality scorecard approach, where members of the organization leadership complete scorecards on the quality provided by their consulting partners. Under certain conditions, some organizations even provide quality bonuses for a job well done. The same concepts above can also apply to knowledge transfer."

"A final component," Mike said, "is to have quality assessments performed by an independent entity who specializes in quality assessments. Given how much we are planning on investing in this initiative, this may be a worthwhile expense to mitigate some of the risks that traditionally accompany initiatives of this scale."

Some Tips on Negotiating

Mike was glad to see that they were covering a lot of the topics he and Jonas had spoken about during their preparation phase. Jonas had further cautioned Mike, "In addition to everything we have talked about so far, there a few risks to consider in your final negotiations of your master statement of work. I am not going to go through all of these, but a few key ones to call out include providing clear processes on handling scope creep and change requests, avoiding currency fluctuations by using one standard currency in your contract, and building provisions around key personnel changes during your program."

"On the flip side, the consulting organization should be protecting themselves from the same scope creep, approval delays—which we just discussed—and a really big one: third-party performance issues. Your risk/reward structures could get pretty muddied up on account of other third parties not performing as expected. Make sure you clearly define the rules of engagement for situations such as this."

"That's all easy to say," Mike had told Jonas. "But it seems like actually getting these in the negotiation process is a whole other animal than us talking about it."

"Of course," Jonas had agreed. "Let me give you some additional perspective that may help you when you're actually trying to carry out these ideas: It's all about having a win-win deal for both parties, or you are just better off having no deal at all, right? Focus on the partnership and sharing the risks and rewards of *mutual success.* The overall goal is to work as one team throughout the negotiations not 'us vs. them.' Not only will this help throughout the negotiation, but it sets the precedence to your delivery teams to do the same throughout the implementation.

"Be sure to go over those risks factors we discussed and any others that you may come up with. Make sure you have clearly defined mitigation strategies documented in your SoW should they materialize.

"And, finally, establish an operating framework that puts all parties in the best possible position to succeed. Always remember: win-win—or no deal."

CHAPTER 11

The Selection

"He's just a jerk," Adhira Das, one of Extron's best integration developers, grumbled.

Mike had his own impressions of Chet as well. As a solution architect, Chet was absolutely brilliant. He could figure out things faster than anyone Mike had ever seen, knew Extron's integrated environment better than anyone else, and could deliver excellent results in nearly half the time as others in his area of specialty.

However, Mike had personally found him difficult to work with in the past and had heard of similar experiences around the water cooler as well. Mike likened Chet to the brilliant heart surgeon with no bedside manner. He was an absolute jerk to deal with, but if you needed a heart transplant, there was no one else you would want to do the surgery.

In Mike's new role, however, it wasn't about how he felt about Chet; it was how his team and the overall program felt about Chet, so he was definitely interested in what Adhira thought.

"So Adhira, why do you think Chet is a Jerk?" he asked.

"Well, he's always just so rude. It's like he thinks he's better than everybody else. His emails are always phrased like he thinks you're an idiot or a child.

In meetings, he's just flat rude to people, cutting them down. He doesn't share information—like he's protecting his turf. Even when he gives someone a compliment, it's backhanded, like he can't bear to say nice words."

Mike had noticed many of these things. Chet was always bucking the way things were done—in the program, in the company. He was belligerent in meetings and emails and abrasive with his coworkers and subordinates. Perhaps Chet thought that if he kept information to himself, it made him indispensable, but Mike was beginning to realize why Chet had had trouble advancing within Extron.

"Do you know if others respond to him the same way?" Mike asked.

"Oh, definitely," Adhira said. "We all are tired of being treated this way."

Mike nodded. "I understand," he told Adhira. "I'll talk to him."

* * *

Mike sat down with Chet a few days later. "So, what's this all about," Chet asked, looking around Mike's office. He was sitting with legs and arms crossed, his posture as closed down as his attitude. "I have work to do."

"I know you do," Mike said gently. "We all do. But that's partly why we're here. Some of your co-workers have told me they're experiencing some difficulties and that it's hurting their productivity."

Chet raised one eyebrow. "Complaints, eh?" he grumbled. "Just tell me who it is. I'll straighten them out."

"You know I can't do that, Chet. And, actually, that's not what this is about."

If Chet had seemed resistant before, he was obviously closed down now. "Oh. So, this is one of 'those' talks? I see where this is going."

"Do you?" Mike replied. "Because I'm wondering if we're seeing the same things. I've known you for, what, twelve years? We came up together, Chet, and I've read your performance reviews. You're a bright guy. You get things done. But over and over, it's the same thing."

Chet shook his head and looked off in the corner as he replied, "Yeah, it's always the same BS stuff—that I don't play well with others. Not a team player. Whatever. That's all just soft-minded crap that distracts from getting the real work done."

"You might be able to say that when you're just doing basic work, but with your skills, they've tapped you for advancement," Mike told him. "That means leading other people, helping to get the best out of them, too. That means personal skills."

"Listen, Mike, I know you've gotta do this, but really, it's not an issue. I'm not a social butterfly. So what? Sometimes I'm a little—frank. I get it. I'm from the Bronx. There's no room for all this political correctness stuff over there. That'll get your butt kicked. It's getting to be that a guy can't even say a simple sentence without it getting thrown back in his face."

"Like telling Eirene that she couldn't think her way out of a paper bag even if she wanted to?"

"She told you about that?" Chet asked with at least the decency to be a little ashamed.

"She didn't have to. I heard it from someone who couldn't help but hear it because you said it so loudly." Mike just stared at Chet for a moment, letting the silence push his point. The other man looked uncomfortable.

"Look, Chet, I don't need you to be Mary Poppins, but I do need you to watch your words—and your tone. You do good work, but if your people are so bent out of shape their morale and consequently productivity goes down, we have a problem. We have a problem if they don't like their work environment. They don't deserve that. And what if we start losing people because of the way you treat them? You going to do their work, too?"

Chet looked chagrinned. He nodded, still not making much eye contact. "All right, boss, I get it," he finally said. "I'll tone it down."

"You're going to have to work on these skills, Chet—I don't see any other way around it," Mike told him firmly. "You're better than this. This shouldn't hold you back. You should be getting promotions, moving up. You need to turn this thing around."

Chet got up, sensing he was dismissed by Mike's tone. Mike let him. "Got it," Chet replied. "You won't hear another peep about me—I got it."

"Good," Mike said to Chet's back as he walked out the door.

Carlos

About a month after the budget planning meeting, they had been able to use the negotiation techniques and scoring models Jonas had helped coach them through to come up with a vendor to be the primary system integrator. They had selected Gley & Stratton, a well-known name in the industry, to essentially help deliver the digital transformation program and another smaller boutique vendor, Covice, to help with the data migration and data governance aspects of the program.

Carlos Arroyo was part of the program management office team immediately brought on board by Gley & Stratton to get pre-planning going. Jonas was surprised and excited to hear that he was on the program. He remembered Carlos from another program he was on where Gley & Stratton was the systems integrator. Though Jonas didn't have a vote in the final decision, he thought that Extron made an excellent choice in Gley & Stratton. All of the final firms were excellent, but the one key differentiator that Gley & Stratton had that the others didn't was the software package they used to help manage their implementations, AMIGO, and Carlos was a passionate advocate for its use.

Jonas said he'd seen the power of AMIGO with another client and was really impressed with its capabilities and had mentioned that to Charles when the CIO brought him on board. Jonas told Mike that he felt that by choosing Gley & Stratton, it removed a few of the potential obstacles of adopting AMIGO as the platform to manage everything that was going to take place on this digital transformation program, as well as position Extron to have a toolset for their future to manage every initiative they would ever have from this point forward.

Mike liked Carlos right away—he was a real salt-of-the-earth kind of guy who didn't sugarcoat or talk in politically correct language that made what he really meant hard to understand. He seemed genuine and highly competent.

One of the first things that Carlos helped Mike with was getting their program onboarding processes up-to-speed for the hundred-plus consultants that would be arriving on campus over the next few weeks. Mobilizing teams of this size so that they were adding value as soon as they onboard was a unique skill set, and Carlos was a master at it.

Carlos also spent a considerable amount of time providing Mike with a detailed walkthrough on the functionality and power of their AMIGO implementation platform. Though Mike conceptually grasped the value that this platform could provide during Gley & Stratton's oral presentation, seeing it firsthand and all its capabilities was really impressive. He knew right away that this tool was going to make his already very complicated job a lot easier to manage.

CHAPTER 12

Communications Management

Now that the program was now off and running and into the initial planning and execution talks, like communications planning and measurement, Mike had started to get a sinking feeling in his gut. The program was going to have a lot of moving pieces going on at once. He had started thinking about all of the different roles and the overall organizational structure they were putting together for the initiative. There were over twenty-five integrated projects, over seventy-five different program roles, and over three hundred resources working around the world—just on this program. Not to mention all of the other stakeholder groups and individual stakeholders that were not *on* the program but still need to be kept in the loop throughout the initiative.

It was completely overwhelming.

"How are we going to communicate with all these individuals, roles, and stakeholder groups, and how are all these different groups and individuals going to communicate with each other?" Mike asked Carlos and Jonas as they walked into his office. They were discussing communications management, and Mike was overwhelmed by the scope of the transformation project.

Jonas answered: "Communications management is an essential process for ensuring that your digital transformation program is sending clear, specific messages to the right constituents, at the right time, with the right medium, and with measurable results."

"I understand that you've got to have communication skills," Mike said, slightly frustrated. "I've been working on being a better active listener, building relationships based on trust and respect, picking up on non-verbal cues, setting priorities, and all the rest, but it's the *how* that I don't understand. There have got to be hundreds of stakeholders who need to share data."

Carlos smiled. "I can help with that—or rather, AMIGO can. We'll work on a more formal communications management process, and I can also share some tips and techniques I use for what I call 'tactical communications'—those very internal and detailed communications that often get missed on large scale initiatives due to project-based silos, geography, and missed integration conversation opportunities."

"It almost sounds like you were waiting for this," Mike grumbled lightly.

"Let's just say it's a very common problem—one that rolling out AMIGO is going to help with a lot," Carlos replied. "You need a toolset that will not only allow you to set up a formal communications plan and process, but also help you connect the communication dots for all of the micro communications that need to occur during an enterprise transformation like this program that usually don't occur and cause a tremendous amount of pain and aggravation. That's what is designed into AMIGO—all transformations have these needs in common."

Formal Communication Management

Mike asked, "How is any company supposed to identify and manage the zillions of communications flying back and forth? There are so many moving parts already—and we're only going to have more."

"First," Carlos began, "we need to define what we're trying to accomplish."

Mike had found that, like Jonas, Carlos had this way of encapsulating topics they needed to cover and opening his understanding. He had to settle in, though; it was a little like some of his favorite professors from college. They could take a while in their lectures, but when you were done, you really understood.

Carlos went on, "As part of our formal communications management, we are launching a set of processes to ensure timely and appropriate generation, collection, storage, retrieval, and ultimate distribution of program information, correct?"

"Right," Mike confirmed. "This is what AMIGO does, right?"

"Exactly. So, the processes for managing stakeholder communications provide the critical links between the stakeholders and the pertinent information that's necessary for successful communication. Through stakeholder communications management, we aim to do about six things:

"First, we need to build awareness and understanding of the digital transformation initiative and the impact it has on the success of the overall organization. Next, we need to communicate that there is dedicated support from the program for engaging communications and that communication is a critical success factor in your transformation.

"Then, we need to establish a living process that will be updated periodically during the program lifecycle as well as based on feedback captured during the process. We also want to ensure that all stakeholder groups receive the appropriate communications in a timely fashion, and we want to establish a repository of all standard communications as a mechanism to help ensure that all stakeholder groups receive the appropriate communications in a timely fashion.

"Finally, we want to address the human components of communication and understanding by ensuring our messaging addresses the six critical questions for communication success:

▶ What is changing?

▶ Why is it changing?

▶ How will I be impacted?

▶ What's in it for me?

▶ What do you need for me to do?

▶ How will I get the knowledge, skills, and information I need?"

Stakeholders

"Just so long as it's not complicated or anything," Mike quipped.

"Oh, it's crazy complicated. That's why companies need our services, and AMIGO helps so much," Carlos replied, not rising to the bait. "So, remember, a stakeholder is an individual, group, or organization, who may affect, be affected by, or perceive itself to be affected by a decision, activity, or outcome of a digital transformation."

Jonas leaned in intently and interjected, "Key stakeholders can make or break the success of your digital transformation. Even if all the deliverables are met and the objectives are satisfied, if your key stakeholders aren't happy, nobody's happy. There are many, many stakeholders and stakeholder groups that will fall into this category when it comes to your digital transformation. It will be your job to identify them and take them through the journey of your digital transformation by providing them the key messages to engage them and gain their loyalty for what you are trying to accomplish."

"How in the world do I *do that*? You make this stuff sound so easy."

"You break it down, piece by piece, Mike," Jonas said patiently. "There are four core sub-processes to our overall communications management process."

"Okay."

"First, there is stakeholder and communications planning, which involves identifying your initiative's stakeholders and determining their information and communication needs." Jonas ticked items off four fingers as he talked. "Second, there are information distributions, which focus on defining the best ways to distribute information to your stakeholders in a timely and appealing manner. Third, there is performance reporting, which focuses on the feedback loop that needs to be put in place to measure overall engagement with your stakeholders. And fourth, there is stakeholder management, which is about the continuous process improvement around messaging and addressing the outliers and issues that occur as a result of communications."

"So, one piece at a time," Mike said, seeing where Jonas was going.

"This is why I tried to impress on you the importance of selecting a good communications team," Jonas said.

Carlos jumped in, "AMIGO will do the heavy lifting, but first, we have to establish the system. Members of your communications team will work with you to identify and review all of the different communications and determine several factors about each one:

▶ What is the communication?

▶ When will it be used (project phase, production release, software version, application environment, etc.)?

▶ What type of communication is it?

▶ What method should be used to send the communication?

▶ Who's responsible for developing the communication?

▶ How often does the communication need to be distributed?

"As part of your communications plan, you will also need to identify the level of engagement each of your stakeholders should have with your digital transformation initiative."

"What do you mean 'level of engagement'?" Mike asked.

"For example, does your stakeholder group just need to be *aware* of what is going on with your initiative because they are not directly impacted by it? For them, having general knowledge of the communication would be helpful, right?"

"Yeah, okay—it might help, but maybe it's not essential."

Carlos nodded. "Or does your stakeholder group need *full understanding and acceptance* of your digital transformation? These stakeholder groups are usually directly impacted by the communication, but they do not have a role in executing the processes surrounding your digital transformation. These stakeholder groups support or provide guidance to the stakeholders directly involved in executing and using the new transformation systems and tools. These could be your business unit leaders who need to understand and send messages to their organizations about the strategic importance of your digital transformation initiative."

"All right, I see what you mean," Mike said, nodding. "Not everyone needs to know everything."

"Another level of engagement is referred to as 'delivering.' This level of engagement is for those stakeholder groups who are directly involved in and responsible for executing the processes supported by your digital transformation. Examples include your power users and end-users.

"But that's not all. Another component of your communication plan is defining the communication medians that will be used to relay your communications. They can be as tactical as standard project update meetings and as sophisticated as social media campaigns and everything in between. The key here is to identify all of the media streams you will require to engage your stakeholders and get them to buy in and transform with you on your digital transformation journey."

Mike pinched the bridge of his nose, feeling a headache coming on. "All our 'streams' seem to be one big, muddy river right now."

"We'll get you through it," Carlos said, encouragingly. "This is nothing unusual, Mike. Do you think it just magically happens at other companies? This is just how the process goes. Once you have all of these components identified, it really is a matter of building a robust matrix of all the different intersecting points, which becomes your tactical communications plan or as what I like to call it, your communications register. AMIGO is going to help a lot with all these things after we get everything set up and moving."

"I know we have gone through a few demos on this already, Carlos, but in a nutshell, what is AMIGO?" Mike asked.

Carlos answered, "AMIGO, which stands for Accelerated Migration and Implementation Governance Office, is a SAAS-based platform that provides unparalleled optics, organization, and connectivity throughout the entirety of a digital transformation initiative. AMIGO has been designed to save large-scale enterprise transformation programs millions of dollars in resource capital reductions, unintegrated software savings, risk reduction, and, most importantly, the avoidance of program resource 'disconnection' that often leads to schedule delays, budget overruns, program collapse, and in the worst of situations, all-out company failure."

"All of which we don't want," Mike exclaimed.

Information Distribution

Carlos launched back out, "Once you have your communication plan in place, you now focus your attention on executing that plan. Information distribution involves making the information described in your plan available to your stakeholders in the medium desired and in a timely manner. Information distribution includes the execution of the plan plus reacting to unexpected or unplanned requests for information.

"The primary inputs for information distribution are the identified stakeholder groups, the identified communication events, and the association of communication events to the stakeholders. All of this information is stored and maintained in your communications register."

"Can you tell me a little more about these unexpected or unplanned requests for information?" Mike asked. "How do you plan for those?"

"Unfortunately, we live in a world that changes, and those changes drive unplanned requests for information. Members of your communication team should capture these requests and concerns and log them in either your program's issues log or action items register, which are also features in AMIGO. From there, the standard-issue management or action items process will be followed, and the subsequent corrective action(s) will be executed to accommodate the request."

"All right," Mike said, nodding, "that seems to make sense. But how do we know if we're communicating effectively? I mean, I'm sure AMIGO is great, but we've got a lot of moving pieces here."

"That's where performance reporting comes in," Carlos answered. "Performance reports measure just how well we did or are doing in terms of our overall communications plan. There are a variety of ways to measure the performance of your communication plan. Some are very tactical easy to get, while others can be a little more challenging without the proper tools in place.

"Think of it like your office thermostat; you want to know if your communication plan is at the perfect temperature. What five questions should you be able to answer to know if your communication is effective?"

Mike thought for a minute. "We need to make sure the right person got it."

Carlos nodded. "Given that email and meetings are still the primary form of business communication, step one is to know that your communication was received. This can be easily tracked through technology or just taking attendance at your meetings. What else?"

"Maybe when they got it?"

"Agreed. Everything in our world today is time-sensitive, so when was your information accessed is critical. If you are communicating a key event to one of your stakeholder groups, you need to know when they are accessing your information. You need to have real-time analytics that point you to the date and time of interaction with your communication. What's next?"

Mike shook his head. "I'm not sure."

"Since our target audiences respond to different methods of communication, and—as part of our plan—we laid out a variety of mediums in which to disseminate information, you need to be able to measure which pieces of your communication was opened, by which medium, and how it was consumed. It is not good enough to only know *if* someone received your information. You need to know if they *understood* the information and if they can act on it."

"So, they need to not just get it—they need to understand it," Mike said slowly. "I follow you."

Carlos told him, "A vital piece for you to measure: Did my recipients understand what I was saying? Face to face, you can read people's body language, but in the digital world, surveys and feedback are the best forms of measurement. Check your recipients' understanding by including a quick survey to solicit their feedback and check their reactions and comprehension. Your survey doesn't need to be lengthy. You can often know by just a few quick multiple-choice, true or false, Likert scale, or short answers where your audience stands!

"Another way to measure understanding and gain retention is through gamification. There are software platforms, like Ringorang, that can help make your communications fun while embedding the essence of your communication and ultimate transformation into the psyche of your stakeholder audience. Can you guess what all that lets you do?"

Mike thought. "Well, I guess it would let us improve our methods of communicating."

Carlos smiled. "To really close the loop on measuring how effective your plan is, you must continuously improve how you share information. Nothing is static. Each time you convey information to either a new or existing audience, their responses may change. Analyze what worked and what didn't and make necessary pivots in your plan.

"As part of this improvement process, and in conjunction with your program's quality assurance process, your communications team can deploy the lessons learned and corrective action plan after each major program phase within your digital transformation initiative. These lessons learned and corresponding corrective action plans can lead to additional stakeholder groups in which to communicate, additional standard communications, and changes to your overall communications register."

"I've heard you talk about managing stakeholders. Can you tell me more about that?" Mike asked. "Some of them are above my pay grade; how do I manage *them*?"

"You know, that's an excellent question, Mike," Jonas pipped up, nodding. "Let me clear something up. While managing stakeholders is the final sub-process of the formal communications management process, we're actually referring to managing the communications to satisfy the needs of, and resolve issues with, your stakeholders. If members of your program are actively managing their stakeholder communications, there is a greater probability that your program will not be derailed due to stakeholder issues, misinformation, or disruptions."

"Sounds good. How do we go about doing that?"

Carlos replied, "There are some tactical ways to manage one's stakeholders through the use of reports generated from your communication register in AMIGO. As issues, concerns, misinformation, etc. occur throughout your program, you can log those concerns in your program's issues register, which is also in AMIGO. These types of issues or tasks will be used to document stakeholder concerns and help maintain a good, constructive working relationship among the various stakeholders within your initiative."

Jonas added, "But don't forget the human side of the equation. Remember, we are dealing with human beings, and not everything can be statistically held in check."

"Right," Mike agreed. "We've got to accept that humans don't always behave in a rational, reasonable, consistent, or predictable way and operate with an awareness of human feelings and potential personal agendas."

"By understanding the root cause of stakeholder behavior, you can assess whether there is a better way to work together to maintain a productive relationship," Jonas told him.

"Any thoughts on the best way to do that?"

"Develop relationships with your stakeholders, which results in increased trust. And where there is trust, people work together more easily and effectively. Investing effort in identifying and building stakeholder relationships can increase confidence across the project environment, minimize uncertainty, and speed problem solving and decision-making.

"Use foresight to anticipate hazards, and use that foresight to take simple and timely actions with stakeholders. Doing so can significantly improve your program delivery. Consider going through a risk management exercise to see where communications could derail and develop proactive strategies to avoid those crossroads."

"Okay," Mike replied.

"Lastly, there is the opportunity for compromise. Establish the most acceptable baseline across a set of stakeholders' diverging expectations and priorities. Assess the relative importance of all stakeholders to establish a sweet spot of alignment among the stakeholder groups, your program, and your sponsorship."

The Secret Sauce

Carlos leaned forward. "So, we've talked about all these stakeholders, and you are beginning to understand just how many there are. All these groups and individuals who need to share information—how do you manage all these communications?

"Now think about the myriad of activities that goes on day-to-day within these groups and how hard each group is working to deliver their plans to make your digital transformations work without a hitch. How often are these stakeholder groups interacting with one another? At what level are they interacting? Are there integrated core activities that are the cornerstone of your transformation initiative that go without even as much as an email conversation?

"If you ran the numbers, you would discover that there are literally thousands of communication points across your program and across these stakeholder groups that *never happen*. What kind of impact does this have?"

Mike could see it wasn't a rhetorical question. Carlos really wanted him to think about this. "Well, I suppose the results could be everything from incidental to chronic problems to crises, depending. It's hard to gauge with a communication that *didn't* happen."

"And *why* didn't they happen?" Carlos pressed.

Mike thought for a moment. "I suppose that those conversations either had no way of happening, because the stakeholders couldn't connect, or they got lost in the shuffle of thousands of communications going every which way."

Jonas soberly said, "In my experience, I have seen missed communications cost companies millions of dollars in program delays. Nothing was done intentionally to sabotage things. Everyone was working their tails off to deliver— it's just that the cross communications were not happening, which caused disconnects in the solution, which inadvertently delayed the launch because of the risk to the organization."

"And time is money," Mike replied. "So how do we avoid that happening? Or minimize it?"

Carlos answered, "I asked myself that for years. How can we learn from failures such as these? We need robust tactical communications within our internal stakeholder groups to avoid million dollars losses and delays?"

"And?" Mike prompted. "What conclusions did you reach?"

"Jonas has talked to you about RACI, right?" Carlos asked. Mike nodded. "And the approach of assigning responsibility, accountability, consulted members, and informed members to each of our work packages, which are associated with one of our deliverables?"

Mike nodded again, and Carlos went on, "Having those relationships goes a long way in keeping the communications clear across the tactical delivery of your work packages, as all RACI members have a built-in network for communications.

"But how do we *keep* the communications flowing among work packages and deliverables that are related to one another? How does a RACI team that's working on a process-related deliverable knowingly keep the communication lines open to a RACI team working on a data deliverable, or an interface deliverable, or a piece of related training? The answer lies in what we refer to as the object relationship."

Mike asked, "What's an 'object relationship?'"

"In the world of technology, an object refers to a combination of variables, functions, and data structures. Today's technology-driven programs may commonly make references to customer, product, vendor, assets, ledger accounts, orders, resources, you name it. These references can all be categorized as different 'objects' within our digital transformation implementation program's domain. With me so far?"

"Ok, so an object is some combination of variables, functions, and data structures among customers, products, vendors, or whatnot. I'm tracking."

"Good," Carlos said, getting excited. "As we are defining the scope of our programs through our work breakdown structures, we are also (albeit indirectly) *defining* those objects that will be in scope for our program. You will discover a myriad of relationships amongst a lot of the information we will be eventually tracking in our overall program."

Jonas jumped in, "We've discussed the hierarchical relationships through organization, portfolios, programs, projects, deliverables, and work packages, but what about those other things that are part of a program? Think about the fundamentals of an integrated core. Within the core, we have budgets, issues, risks, actions, key decisions, change requests, communications itself, knowledge, quality, and, most importantly, *people*."

Carlos nodded, taking over. "All of the details surrounding these fundamentals can be tied to objects. And by tying each of these details to objects, and by having RACI members tied to our work packages, which are tied to these objects, we now can connect the dots across our entire initiative and build a network map of all the moving parts and connection points that need to be communicated."

"Carlos," Mike said as he began to understand what the older man was saying. "That's brilliant!"

"Now, this would be a lot to put into a communications register," Carlos said with a chuckle.

"Can you imagine a communications register with about a million communication lines?" Jonas asked.

Carlos just shook his head at the thought. "From a human perspective, it would be impractical—*impossible*—to try to maintain all of these communication lines and keep the communications coordinated, but with technology, we can build these network maps and handle all these thousands of communications."

"AMIGO?"

Carlos nodded, smiling broadly. "Yes, AMIGO."

"It's definitely going to be your best friend," Jonas added.

CHAPTER 13

The Surgeon

Mike and Nancy sat together in the surgeon's waiting room. The entire practice was tastefully decorated, and Nancy had busied herself during the wait by walking around and looking at some of the decorations and chatting about them with the waiting room receptionist. Everything was in themes of pink, with recurring breast cancer-pink ribbons. Dr. Janet Smith was one of the most well-regarded breast cancer surgeons in their area and was noted for being the top woman in her field. Nancy had picked her to head up her cancer treatment team, and now they were at the final office meeting before Nancy would get her surgery.

Mike still couldn't believe it—couldn't believe they were sitting in this room, that Nancy had cancer, that she'd have to get surgery to remove the cancer—none of it. Sometimes, it seemed like it was happening to someone else, and he was simply riding along inside that person's head as an observer, watching a movie, rather than as the one in control of his actions and words. He just felt numb.

Nancy, for her part, had once again demonstrated that she was not only likely the nicest person Mike had ever known but also perhaps the strongest. After the initial shock, she'd cried and mourned, and then she'd gone into action. She began to research, talk to friends and loved ones who'd dealt with cancer, and arm herself with facts and information about treatment options, physicians, hospitals, and more. Mike thought a lesser woman would've hidden under the covers and waited for decisions to be forced on her or have had other people lead her by the hand. Not Nancy. She'd grieved—they grieved together, both shedding plenty of tears—and then she'd moved.

Cancer had better watch out. Nancy was coming for it!

Dr. Smith was a tall, no-nonsense kind of woman without a lot of bedside manner. When she walked into their exam room about half an hour after they arrived, she quickly laid out the facts.

"Your biopsies both came back positive," she said bluntly. "That's bad, because it shows the cancer has moved from the original site in the left breast and affected this lymph node, and if it's in that one, it is likely in others. That means we can officially say that you are Stage III, and you may know from any reading on the internet that Stage III means we must work very hard and very diligently, *now*, if you want to make it through this."

Hearing the surgeon speak like this made Mike's stomach curl up into a ball and drop like a lead weight into his guts. He shot a glance at Nancy, who was tightly controlled, obviously frightened, but engaging fully with Dr. Smith.

"What does that mean for treatment?" she asked.

Dr. Smith made a sour face. "It means we use everything at our disposal. For your case, I want to perform surgery first. We will go in, and I will remove the tumor and a number of lymph nodes around it. Hopefully, we can get clean margins—meaning I can remove the tumor cleanly from the tissues on your chest wall—and the full modified mastectomy will remove the cancerous tissues completely. At that point, you'll work with an oncologist—I recommend Dr. Nusbaum—on an aggressive chemotherapy regimen designed to kill any remaining cancerous cells throughout your body. At Stage III, our big concern is that it could be headed elsewhere, and we must stop it now. I suggest you then start a round of radiation—I like Dr. Heaton."

"All of that?" Nancy asked in a small voice.

A trace of humanity slipped into Dr. Smith's disposition as she leaned in closer to Nancy. "Understand, Mrs. Bennett, you have a very aggressive form of cancer. It is a very common type, estrogen-progesterone positive, and we have a great deal of research and established treatment protocols. However, just because we know a great deal about it, do not misunderstand—it is very serious. Because it is aggressive, we must also be aggressive."

Nancy asked a few more questions. The doctor said a few more things. Mike even heard himself ask about something, but it was like he was hearing his own voice from far away, and his numbed feeling of disconnection lasted until they were partway home.

"That was—intense," he finally said, struggling to find words that wouldn't make the appointment seem worse or more discouraging than it was but that also accounted for the gravity.

"I like her," Nancy told him.

"You do?" Mike asked.

She nodded. "No false promises, no empty clichés, just down to business. That woman fights death every day. She cuts it away with a little tiny sword on a surgery table."

Mike hadn't thought of it that way. What would that do to someone over time? Surely not all her patients made it—Mike didn't want to go there, didn't want to entertain that thought, so he pushed it away.

"Well, if you like her, that's enough for me," he said lamely.

CHAPTER 14

Risk Management

Mike dropped Nancy back at home and headed for the office for a few hours as Jonas was coming over for a meeting with Charles and wanted to catch up with Mike as well.

After some small talk about his meeting with Charles, Jonas jumped right into what he wanted to talk to Mike about today.

"Have I talked to you about the difference between risks and issues?" Jonas asked. Given Mike's morning with Nancy, he was thinking, "Risks and Issues, how appropriate."

"Maybe," Mike muttered. He honestly couldn't remember. "I'm a little disconnected this afternoon, Jonas. You might have to help me out here."

Jonas understandably replied, "A risk is an uncertain event or condition, that—if it occurs—has a positive or negative effect on the program's objectives. An issue is a point or matter that is in dispute, or an unsettled point or matter with opposing points of view."

"Can you give me that in layman's terms, Professor Jonas?" Mike somewhat sarcastically shot back. Jonas, the ever-professional consultant, did not engage in the sarcasm sensing that Mike was having a bad day. "Think of it like this, Mike: A risk is like a steaming pile of dog crap on the path ahead of you. It's an obstacle, but you're trying to figure out how to avoid stepping in it. An issue is when you've already stepped in it, and it's all over your shoe." Hoping to get a smile or chuckle out of Mike.

"Things are looking pretty crappy to me," Mike replied while in the back of his mind thinking how life imitates work at times. Were there things that Nancy could have done to see that cancer was going to be in her life path, and could she have done anything to avoid getting it? Unfortunately, that did not happen, and they now had a "life or death" issue on their hands. A more poignant definition of risk vs. issue.

"Pun intended, no doubt," Jonas said with half a chuckle. "Perhaps all you need is some perspective. So, what's the process for risk management?"

"Risk identification, risk evaluation, risk planning, risk tracking, and monitoring and control," Mike recited. "Jonas, honestly, I appreciate you, but if this is just going to be quiz day, now is not the time."

Jonas made a downward motion with both his open palms, urging Mike to calm down as he said, "I know, I know. I'm going somewhere with this. Indulge me just a little? I think it will be worth it."

Mike took a deep breath. Jonas had become a friend and was definitely an invaluable part of the process. "Ok, Jonas. I'm sorry; I'm on a short fuse right now."

"I get it," Jonas said, sounding like he genuinely cared. "This will help."

"Okay."

Risk Identification

Jonas said, "During the risk identification stage, we are trying to identify all the different risks that can either positively or negatively impact our program or the organization as a direct result of our program. What we try to do as part of this process is think about these risks across a variety of 'big rocks,' or areas that you typically need to view as part of risk identification.

"Talent," Jonas said, ticking off one of five fingers. "From the top of the organization down to the user team members, talent is a primary risk and success factor. In this case, talent not only refers to that which is applied to the program, but also the behavior and attitude one has in their engagement within the program.

"Program management—transformation efforts are inherently complex with thousands of deliverables and decisions. Program processes related to governance, risk treatment, and communications are directly correlated with program execution performance and tactical benefit attainment.

"Next comes methods—methods refer to the methodology or methodologies you use to execute your digital transformation program. A well designed, coordinated set of methods is essential to deliver a high-quality set of capabilities and to ensure they are utilized as planned. The methods you use on your program should be integrated and proven to reduce risk of rework and false starts.

"Technology—software is simply a tool, but a very important one. It's a tool that needs to be supported by an adequate infrastructure to allow for acceptable performance. The technology must also be robust enough to deal with future collaboration and security requirements.

"Last is environmental—risks in delivering a successful program are often outside of the control of the program manager but still must be monitored and escalated appropriately. Risks in this category tend to be the responsibility of the steering or sponsorship body of the program."

"But those are really big, general categories," Mike noted. "How do we break these down into smaller 'rocks' so we can make it more manageable?"

"We can sub-compartmentalize your risk identification thought process,"[9] Jonas agreed. "The goal of the exercise I want to show you is to think through all the possible risks that can hit your program. This is not a 'one and done' exercise. This is something you will continue to do throughout the entire life cycle of your program. However, to help you think through your planning, it is good to spend significant time upfront while you are doing your initial preparation for the program as this will help you in the development of your initial program plans and budget—which you have."

"Well, I've tried," Mike muttered. "Not sure how successful I've been."

"One of the challenges that most people have in risk identification is

---

9 For more information on risk identification, please go to www.platinumpmo.com/thetransformationbook

actually identifying what the true risk really is. A lot of times, people will identify *symptoms* or *causes* that they assume are the risk, but in reality, they are not."

"Okay," Mike acknowledged. "Go on..."

"I learned this technique from one of the foremost experts on risk management.[10] She recommends phrasing your risks in risk statements that follow a sentence structure cadence that goes something like this: As a result of 'X,' there is a risk that 'Y' will occur that will result in 'Z.' 'X' represents what is causing the risk. 'Y' represents the actual risk, and 'Z' represents the consequence should the risk actually occur.

"For example, 'As a result of the upcoming summer holidays, resources may not be available to participate in critical deliverable creation sessions, which would result in delays to the completion of those deliverables as well as the overall program timeline.'"

Mike said, "So, the cause is the upcoming summer holidays, the risk is resource availability, and the consequence is delays to the completion of those deliverables and impacts to the overall timeline."

"Exactly."

"But how do you go about identifying the risks for our program?" Mike asked.

Jonas replied, "You can review your program charter and look for things that jump out at you as possible risks. If your digital transformation initiative has been submitted for bid to some system integrators via a request for proposal, ask them to define their risks as part of their proposal response. You can also review your assumptions—there are usually some risks buried within them. I have also found that just reading articles and whitepapers of what others have gone through on their journeys is a good way to identify risks. And if you are part of any professional associations, discuss their experiences with colleagues. I am sure by exploring these options, you will be able to define a bunch of risks."

"I'm sure I can," Mike agreed. "What next?"

---

10 Rita Mulcahy was an author and public speaker in the Project Management field. She was the founder and CEO of RMC Project Management and an internationally recognized expert on project management techniques, advanced project management theory, risk management and the Project Management Professional Exam.

Risk Evaluation

"After you've defined some risks, your next step is risk evaluation. As part of this stage, you are evaluating risks on their probability of occurrence and the impact the risk would actually have on your program should it actually materialize. If you have a boatload of risks to evaluate, you may want to provide a high-level qualitative assessment of the risks. This can be as simple as providing a high-medium-low ranking of the probability and impacts. This will help you prioritize your large list of risks you identified and help you to focus on the high-highs, the high-mediums, the medium-highs, etc."

"So, you can tackle the most dangerous ones first."

"Once you have done the *qualitative* analysis, you can go into the detailed *quantitative* analysis. You can set up your own ratings and assessments, but I like a ten-point system myself. It all depends on the granularity you want for your program. A good rule of thumb is to always try to *dollarize* your risks. In other words, should this risk materialize, how much will it cost me in dollar value or time (which can be calculated into dollar value)? Program leaders are always looking for tangible and quantifiable measures. Now, I know that not all risks can be measured this way, but to the extent that you can, it will help you in your future conversations with your leadership around budgets."

"Makes sense," Mike commented. His headache seemed to be feeling better, and his mood was improving with it. "What next?"

"Once you have performed your quantitative analysis and have defined your probability and impact scores, you can plot those scores on what is called a risk heat map.[11] The risks that fall in the red zone should receive the greatest attention. These risks (if they occur) will have the greatest negative impact on the program. Those risks that fall in the yellow zone should have a mitigation plan and should be monitored. Those risks that fall in the green zone should be monitored ongoing for potential increase in risk. We usually put these on a risk watchlist."

"What about exposure?" Mike asked. "I'm more familiar with that."

"That's another calculation we want to perform. Risk exposure is a

---

11 For more information on risk heat maps, please go to www.platinumpmo.com/thetransformation-book

scoring mechanism that takes the probability of the risk occurring multiplied by the impact that risk would have should it occur. If you tie the risk exposure to the risk heat map, any risk exposure score 4 or greater is red, 2.1—3.9 is yellow, less than 2.1 would be in the green zone."

Risk Planning

Jonas was on a roll. "Once you've finished evaluating your risk, you want to go to the next stage, which is risk planning. In this stage, we are trying to determine the most appropriate course of action to minimize or eliminate the threat, or in the case of opportunities, maximize the opportunity to the program. As part of risk planning, the first thing we want to do is establish a risk response, which is the work performed to assess options and actions to enhance opportunities and reduce threats.

"There are traditionally four risk responses we can choose:

> ▶ We can avoid the risk by taking action to steer around it to eliminate the threat entirely.

> ▶ We can accept the risk and just deal with the consequences should the risk materialize.

> ▶ We can transfer the risk by shifting the negative impacts to a different party to put ownership on someone else.

> ▶ Or we can mitigate the risk by designing a plan to minimize the threat by reducing its probability and/or impact."

"How do you know which to do?" Mike asked.

"A good rule of thumb to follow would be if your risk is in the yellow or red zone and your risk response is to accept, you will most likely need to create a contingency plan—which is developed in advance as a course of action should the risk materialize.

"Do you remember my analogy and pictures of the differences between a risk and an issue? Imagine if you were on your way to the most important job interview of your life, and the only way of getting to that job interview was to walk through a dog kennel. What we are talking about here are situations where stepping in the dog doo-doo might be unavoidable.

"In these cases, we want to have a contingency plan well in advance. In our ridiculous example, having a handy way to wash your shoes—or another set of shoes entirely—would be a good contingency plan. In all seriousness, this is a really important point. You don't want to be having to think about these things when the dog stuff is hitting the fan."

As Jonas was giving his analogy, Mike was thinking of real life. What if the radiation didn't shrink the tumor enough? What if the cancer spread to all of the lymph nodes? What if chemo destroys Nancy's will to live? What if Nancy *died*? Mike's head was just swirling in thoughts, negative emotions, and, unfortunately, contingency plans.

As Mike had this track of despair running through the back of his head, Jonas continued on, "Early in my career, I was leading a large warehouse software implementation. We did all of our planning, ran mock cutovers, and had our implementation down pat. Though there was a risk of the implementation not going well, we really didn't think much about that happening, or the ramifications should it actually happen.

"So, we started our warehouse software implementation, which was a twenty-four-hour implementation plan that required bringing down the warehouse for twenty-four hours. The plan and execution went flawlessly, and we got the warehouse back up and running right on schedule.

"About four hours into the first shift, we noticed that the software was not working well. After six hours, we had major problems. After eight hours, it was a disaster, and the organization leadership decided to roll-back the implementation and revert back to the old software. The problem was, we never developed a contingency plan for that event. We knew it was possible, but we just never really thought it through.

"Now imagine the situation. You've been up thirty-six straight hours now implementing a new software solution, and now you have to come up with a plan to back it out. Not a good time to be thinking it through. If I had developed my contingency plan in advance, I would have been prepared when my software implementation hit the fan, and we could have calmly followed our roll-back plan.

"The point of this conversation is you don't want to be thinking and planning these types of situations in times of crisis. You want to have a game plan when the stuff hits the fan. And that is why you need contingency plans for those really big risks."

Jonas explained, "One of the things you want to do as part of your risk planning effort is calculating your program's risk reserves. This is something that you want to focus us during your program's preparation activities, as it will really help you with your initial budgeting.

"There are two buckets of risk reserves: your contingency reserves and your management reserves. The contingency reserve is the reserve that you, as the program manager, have the most control over. What we are looking to do is quantify and dollarize your 'known-known' risks and risk exposure. This is where that work we did to dollarize our risks during risk evaluation is going to pay off. We'll look at the dollarized value of all of our yellow and red risks and multiply each of those dollar values by its corresponding probability. The sum of all of these dollar values becomes your contingency reserve.

"The management reserve is for those 'unknown-unknown' risks that you just could not foresee happening (because we don't have a crystal ball). This reserve is usually owned by your steering committee and is usually about 10 percent of your budget.

"So, a nice way to finalize your plan and budget for your plan is to take the budget from your critical chain-driven program plan *plus* your defined expenses *plus* the value your contingency reserve *plus* the value of your management reserve."

Mike looked at Jonas as if going through a flashback. "Now that you mention it, we did put some 'oops' money in the budget for contingency. However, I'm not sure if it's enough. It was a SWAG. I am going to work on this and come up with a more statistically generated number to see how close we came to our SWAG figure. This is a really solid approach, Jonas."

"That sounds great, Mike. In hindsight, I'm sorry we didn't have this conversation earlier," Jonas replied apologetically.

Risk Tracking

"Our last stage is risk tracking with monitoring and controlling," Jonas said. "As the name indicates, here is where we are going to track all of our work around our risks.

"We want to look at this from a perspective of auditability. What will your program auditors be looking for in terms of your risk management process? You will create reports to satisfy their needs, as well as the needs of your program leadership and executive steering committee. This is also a good opportunity to integrate with your organization's enterprise risk management group. Utilize your reporting as a conduit to this group. It will help with your overall alignment and buy-in from an organizational perspective."

"That's a really good idea," Mike said, trying to keep his head in the game. "I actually know George Majeres, who leads our enterprise risk management group. Our kids are in soccer club together. It would be a great opportunity to see how they are doing things from an enterprise perspective and build some synergies from our program perspective."

Six Rules of Risk Management

"I believe there are six rules for risk management," Jonas explained, "but this is just my take:

1. Make it a recurring process

2. Identify risks early in your program

3. Communicate about risks

4. Consider both threats and opportunities

5. Don't ignore non-quantifiable risks

6. Address cultural issues that contribute to program risk

"Why is it not enough to do it at program kickoff?" Jonas asked.

"Because things can change," Mike said, understanding.

Jonas nodded. "It's not enough to do it once. You've got to do it repeatedly—make it part of the process. The first rule is essential to the success of program risk management. If you don't truly embed risk management into your program, you cannot reap the full benefits of this approach. You can encounter any number of faulty approaches in companies. Some programs use no approach whatsoever to risk management. They are either ignorant and running their first program, or they are somehow confident that no risks will occur in their program (which of course will happen). Some people blindly trust the program manager, especially if they look like a battered army veteran who has been in the trenches for the last two decades. Professional companies make risk management part of their day-to-day operations and include it in program meetings and the training of staff.

"Next, you want to identify risks early in your program. This tip aligns with our earlier discussion on risk identification. Identifying the risks that are present in your program requires an open mindset that focuses on future scenarios that may occur. Two main sources exist to identify risks—people and paper. People are your team members who each bring along their personal experiences and expertise. Other people to talk to are experts outside your program who have a track record of the type of program or work you are facing, like me. We can reveal some booby traps you will encounter or some golden opportunities that may not have crossed your mind. Interviews and team sessions (risk brainstorming) are the common methods of discovering the risks people know.

"Paper is a different story. Programs tend to generate a significant number of (electronic) documents that contain program risks. They may not always have that name, but someone who reads carefully (between the lines) will find them. The program plan, business case, and resource planning are good starters. Other categories are old program plans, your company's intranet, and specialist websites."

"Are you saying we'll be able to identify all risks before they occur?" Mike asked, slightly incredulous.

Jonas shook his head. "Probably not. However, if you combine a number of different identification methods, you are likely to find the vast majority. If you deal with them properly, you will have enough time left for the unexpected risks that take place."

"So, we could fail from a risk we couldn't identify?"

"Possibly. But I'll tell you this: Failed programs I've observed show that program managers were frequently unaware of the big hammer that was about to hit them. The frightening finding was that frequently, *someone* within the program organization actually *did* see the hammer—but didn't inform the program manager of its existence. If you don't want this to happen in your program, you better pay attention to risk communication."

Mike shuddered slightly. "So, what you're saying is that it's not enough to just try to identify risks if we're not communicating about them."

"Very good," Jonas affirmed. "A good approach is to consistently include risk communication in the tasks you carry out. If you have a team meeting, make program risks part of the default agenda (and not the final item on the list)! This shows risks are important to you and gives team members a *natural moment* to discuss them and report new ones.

"Another important line of communication is that of the program manager and program sponsor or principal. Focus your communication efforts on the big risks here and make sure you don't surprise the boss! Also, take care that the sponsor makes decisions on the top risks because usually some of them exceed the mandate of the program manager."

"So, you're saying that Charles and Arthur Jonesborough might have some high-level decisions to make?"

"Some of these items will be over your pay grade," Jonas agreed. He went on, "So, earlier we talked about risks and issues? Well, risks come in opportunities and threats. You've got to consider both threats and opportunities.

"Program risks have a negative connotation: They are the *bad guys* that can harm your program. However, modern risk approaches also focus on 'positive risks,' the program opportunities. These are the uncertain events that are beneficial to your program and organization. These *good guys* make your program faster, better, and more profitable.

"Unfortunately, a lot of program teams struggle to cross the finish line because they're overloaded with work that needs to be done quickly. This creates a program dynamic where only negative risks matter (if the team considers any risks at all). Make sure you create some time to deal with the opportunities in your program, even if it is only half an hour. The chances are that you will see a couple of opportunities with a high payoff that doesn't require a big investment of time or resources."

"For example," Jonas went on, "I had this situation at one of my clients years ago where they had a division in their organization that was part of the scope of their digital transformation, but it just really didn't 'fit' in terms of form, function, and capability like the other divisions did. So, as a program, we identified an opportunity to descope the division from the implementation and build some interfaces for organization reporting purposes. The opportunity had a projected time savings of about six months and about twelve-million-dollar overall savings. So, we went through the risk/opportunity process with the executive steering committee, and they agreed to remove that division from scope. We were able to reduce our program costs and time to deliver dramatically. And, would you believe it, three years later the organization ended up selling off that division anyway. That opportunity was a good win!"

"So, they just descoped it?" Mike asked. Jonas nodded, and Mike considered the implications of this.

"There is a tendency among program managers to adhere too closely to Peter Drucker's maxim, *'If you can measure it, you can manage it,'*" Jonas said. "But it's important that you don't ignore non-quantifiable risks. This plays out in managers focusing too much on risks they can quantify, often at the cost of non-quantifiable risks. They assume that if you can't quantify the risk, you can't manage it either. This obviously isn't true. Non-quantifiable risks are also manageable but require a different approach. You have to look beyond the data and spot problems in a more holistic manner."

Mike asked, "What do you mean? How do you spot them in a 'holistic' manner?"

Jonas continued, "There are several steps you can take to deal with non-quantifiable risks:

► Make a list of all risks to the program. Then determine the extent *and* the quality of data available for each risk.

► If there isn't enough data about a risk, use industry benchmarks, case studies, and even subjective data such as anecdotes. These might be less reliable, but it's better than going in blind.

► Make a list of KPIs for tracking the performance of the deliverable associated with the risk. Use these KPIs to find indicators that can help you spot chances of failure/success.

► In case of risks with absolutely no data, consider alternative solutions. Two common options are **avoidance** (i.e., scrapping the deliverable altogether) and **transfer** (i.e., offloading responsibility to a third party).

► Make sure that you communicate frequently about non-quantifiable risks. Keeping everyone in the loop can often help you spot non-quantifiable risks early and take evasive measures."

"Earlier, you mentioned cultural issues. What did you mean by that?" Mike asked.

Jonas proceeded carefully. "Digital transformation programs don't exist in isolation. The values and beliefs your organization cherishes trickle down to the bottom. Some of these end up increasing risk in a program."

"How so?"

"For example, the failure of team members to collaborate effectively can derail a program. But if the business does not value collaboration and communication, can you really blame your team members for not prioritizing them either?"

Mike answered reluctantly, "Probably not."

"This is why you have to see program risk management as more than an isolated, program-specific exercise. Instead, you have to paint a wider target. Look beyond the team and consider the cultural issues that contribute to program risks. Ask yourself whether there any values that help or hurt the program.

"You'll need buy-in from executives if you're going to pull it off. Get them involved in the risk management process. Show them how the organization's culture increases the chances of programs failing."

"That sounds," Mike began uncertainly, "difficult."

Jonas nodded. "Solving cultural issues can be an enormous challenge. But it can result in a long-term impact on your company's ability to mitigate program risks."

CHAPTER 15

Issue Management

A couple of weeks after Nancy's consultation with the surgeon, she'd completed her surgery. The first few days were intense. Mike had never seen Nancy in such pain. As hard as he'd tried to play, "Nurse Mike," he knew he needed some help. Mike ended up asking Nancy's mom, Anna, to come down from Minnesota to be with her and help her get around for those first couple of weeks after surgery. That would also give Mike some relief at home while he dealt with his crazy work schedule.

After a few weeks, Nancy started to feel more like herself again. The sharpest pain was over, and now she was working to regain lost mobility. It was rough, but together they'd pulled through. Next up, chemo.

Unfortunately, enterprise digital transformations are not sympathetic to any one person's personal circumstances, and the daily grind of Mike's role in the program never decelerated during this time. Life, and the program, continued to move forward.

One afternoon, Mike and Jonas had a lunch meeting scheduled for the day. The more time Mike spent with Jonas, the more he liked him; the older man had a calming effect. But he was now getting hungry, and they did some of their best talking over food.

"Hey, Mike, ready to grab some lunch?" Jonas asked.

Mike checked his watch. "I could definitely eat—if you're buying."

Jonas, cleverly seizing the moment, replied, "Great, but if I'm buying, then we are going to talk about your 'issues.'"

Mike laughed and replied, "My 'issues'? Which ones?" They laughed together as they got up. Mike asked, "Mexican sound good? I'm craving these taquitos they make by hand at this one place."

"Sounds great," Jonas agreed, and they set off.

"So, our last time together, we were talking about risk," Mike said after they had sat down and ordered. "Dog crap in the road that we don't want to step in. But what if we do?"

"Then you've got issues," Jonas supplied. "Issue management is simply the process of identifying and resolving issues. Problems with staff or vendors, technical failures, integration challenges—these might all negatively impact your project. If the issue goes unresolved, you risk creating unnecessary conflicts, delays, or even failure to produce your deliverables and work packages."

"Not to mention stinky shoes," Mike said, crunching a chip. "So, what does issue management look like?"

Jonas replied, "The issue management process is comprised of five stages: issue identification, issue evaluation, Issue escalation, issue resolution, and issue tracking."

"Sounds straightforward."

Jonas rolled his palm back and forth, indicating a maybe. "It can be. Through the first stage of the issue management process, issue identification, we are trying to document all of those items where we are at an impasse and need resolution: with another team member, another project team, or on a problem with multiple options and no clear choice. Anyone on the program can identify issues. As part of a standard process an issue owner should be identified.

"The issue owner is usually the person who has the most interest in seeing its resolution. This is usually the same person whose deliverables are being impacted by the open issue. Therefore, the issue owner is usually the same person as the person responsible for an impacted deliverable or work package.

"In the olden days, we used to enter issues in an issue log. This was normally done in an Excel workbook. Given the complexity and geography of most digital transformation initiatives, that's why I highly recommended that you deploy a formal online system like AMIGO to help capture and track your program's issues."

"That would be one heck of an Excel document," Mike commented.

"Exactly. So, you identify it and then evaluate it. During the evaluation process, the issue is reviewed and analyzed for potential solutions. This is one of the great things about AMIGO—it has a formal and integrated issue management process as part of the platform that lets all pertinent people know about issues in their domains of interest.

"One key component during the evaluation process is identifying what deliverables this issue is impacting and if any of those deliverables are on the program's critical chain. If an issue is impacting a deliverable that is on or near the program's critical chain, it needs to be dealt with and resolved immediately because that issue is causing a day-for-day slip in the delivery of the overall program, essentially costing thousands of dollars in lost budget to the program."

"Are those 'red' issues?" Mike asked.

Jonas nodded as he loaded a chip up with salsa. "These are your highest priority. The rule of thumb in this situation is to drop everything you are doing and get the right people in a room to resolve this issue immediately."

"But what if you can't resolve the issue immediately?"

"Issues that cannot be resolved or require a higher authority resolution are escalated to the appropriate level within your program. A good leading practice is to provide a recommended resolution for the issue. This serves two purposes: It provides context to a higher-level decision body who may not be as familiar with the issue or its context to the program, and it is used to trigger what is referred to as 'the standard resolution period' for all issues."

"How long is the 'standard' standard resolution period?" Mike asked.

Jonas answered, "You decide. Your program should determine a standard resolution period for all non-critical path issues. If the issue is not resolved within that standard resolution period, then the recommended resolution becomes the final resolution. This process will ensure timely completion of your issues and resolutions and allow individuals to continue to get their deliverables done on schedule."

"So, you're just pre-deciding on how long you're going to give everyone to resolve an issue before moving on?" Mike asked.

"Right," Jonas replied. "Once the recommended resolution is provided, the current owner will document the recommended resolution and provide additional comments as appropriate and then re-assigned the issue to the higher authority for final resolution."

"Did you hear about the one where the project manager was asked to escalate a problem?" Jonas asked.

Confused, Mike shook his head.

"He was confused because he didn't know which escalator to get on," Jonas deadpanned.

Mike groaned.

"But seriously, you want to build a hierarchy of teams in which to escalate to, depending on the severity of the issue. You might have levels such as individual, sub-team, project team, program, advisory board, and executive steering committee. Issues that are impacting individuals within your team are traditionally handled by your team leads. Issues that are impacting more than one team on a project will be handled by your project manager. Issues that are impacting more than one project will be handled by your program manager. Complicated issues outside the program manager's span of influence will be escalated to your program advisory board. Those where the advisory board cannot resolve are escalated to the executive steering committee."

"Does that happen a lot?"

"About 75-80 percent of your issues should be handled at the project level or below, 10-15 percent at the program level, and the rest at the advisory board or executive steering committee level. So, no."

"So, how do we resolve these things?" Mike asked. Their food came and was sizzling hot on the plate. The waitress had to serve them with oven mitts on. It looked amazing. They were both quiet while she laid out the food and then as they tried it.

"The issue resolution process provides the action plan and resolution for the issue," After chewing and swallowing a bite of his chile relleno, Jonas replied, "Once an issue action plan is complete or the issue is resolved by the issue owner, the issue originator is informed of the final resolution. At that point the issue originator can close out the issue.

"One key point is the recommended resolution. If the issue is on the critical chain and the resolution is not finalized by the due date, then the recommended resolution becomes the final resolution."

"Just like that?"

"You've got to decide on something," Jonas replied.

Mike finished another bite. "I guess when it's time to get off the pot, you've got to do *something*."

"The last process in issue management is issue tracking," Jonas said. "During this process, the project managers will ensure that the overall issue process is being executed properly within their team and that documentation of the issues generated from their team follows your program standards. It's through these good documentation practices we will be able to quickly comply with any program audit requests. Additionally, your project managers will perform analysis on the issues associated with their project areas and provide any necessary escalations."

"How often do you suggest going over these?" Mike asked, chewing.

"Program leadership should review standard issues on a weekly basis. The issues that are impacting the program's critical path are dealt with immediately. Don't wait until the next meeting to discuss those. Schedule an emergency meeting with all the appropriate responsible, accountable, and consulted resources for the issue and resolve it immediately."

"Any tips for effective issue management?" Mike asked, grabbing some sour cream for a taquito.

Jonas gave him a "*don't get me started*" look but set his fork down for a moment to think. "Get the categorization system right. Don't kill issues management with convoluted systems. Empower your issue management teams. Resolve issues quickly." He thought for another moment. "Sometimes, you must make decisions among bad alternatives. And look for common causes for multiple issues in a short timeframe."

"Okay," Mike said, thinking. "Where do you start?"

"Get the categorization system right. A list of one hundred issues will just confuse people. Break them down into categories that make sense for your program."

"So, be organized."

"Yes," Jonas answered, "but don't kill issues management with convoluted systems. The more time people spend managing the system, the less time they spend managing the issues. And keep your issues management teams tight and empowered. Place the right people, representing the right functions, around the table. Keep in mind that issues management teams with thirty people will barely manage themselves, let alone the issue. Try using the hierarchical structure I talked to you about."

"A big team like that would never get anything done," Mike agreed.

"You want to resolve issues quickly," Jonas advised. "Issues will impede your program's progress. Therefore, if a problem is indeed being classified as an issue, the program manager must take responsibility for getting it resolved. By the same reasoning, if there is no urgency to resolve the issue or if the issue has been active for some time, you should look again to see if it really *is* an issue. It may be a potential problem (risk), or it may be an action item that needs to be resolved at some later point. By their nature, issues must be resolved with a sense of urgency. A good habit to get into is to measure the velocity in which issues are closed. The quicker, the better."

"Kind of like how we closed this meal," Mike quipped, noting that they'd both nearly cleared their plates.

Jonas laughed. "You want to measure just how quickly issues are being resolved and elevate those metrics to the top of your program management dashboards. It is through the issue resolution velocity (and key decision-making velocity, which we will talk about next) that drives the completion of your deliverables and work packages."

"How do you like to associate your issues?"

"So, as a rule of thumb, be sure your issues are tied to at least the deliverable level if not the work package level so you can identify the blockages to progress on the program and the potential impacts to your critical chain."

"But what about when there *is* no good choice? How can you make a quick decision then?" Mike asked.

"After reviewing the process and the techniques for managing issues, you may think that you should be able to successfully resolve every issue if you only knew the right technique. In fact, you may find some issues that do not have good, clean solutions. In some cases, it may be difficult to determine any good options for resolution. Other times, issues arise that are hard to resolve not because of a lack of options, but because of the difficulty gaining approval and resolution among a number of alternatives. In other cases, you may have a number of options that are less than optimal, and the ultimate resolution may be one that is the 'least offensive.'"

"I don't much like the sound of that. Has this happened to you a lot? Can you think of what has caused this kind of problem?" Mike asked.

Jonas thought carefully. He was no doubt under agreements and had to watch his words. "An example of this dilemma is an issue that involves internal politics. Usually, when a problem starts to get mixed up with internal politics, you will find that the resolution is difficult because there is more to the decision-making process than a cool examination of the facts. When a problem becomes political, in fact, a resolution may be approved that is actually *far* less than optimum for the program team. However, a less-than-perfect solution may be preferable to deadlock or the prospect of an even worse alternative being approved."

"Do you ever encounter related or common problems?" Mike asked.

"Sometimes, you may encounter a number of issues in a short timeframe," Jonas replied. "If this happens on your program, look to see if some are related. If so, try to resolve the issue that looks like more of a root cause. The resolution of this issue may subsequently resolve others. If the issues look independent, try to resolve those with the most negative impact on the program first."

CHAPTER 16

Key Decision Management

Mike ordered sopapillas with honey, which the two men shared. "The challenge I'm seeing," Mike said thoughtfully, "is how, as a program leadership team, do we handle the volume of key decisions that need to be made in a timely fashion to keep my program on the right track? How do I build teams and processes to make those decisions? And how do we make those quality decisions stick?"

"Digital transformation programs can be decision-heavy," Jonas replied. "They're fundamentally different than any other type of project an organization will run."

"Sometimes, I feel like Atlas with the weight of the world on my shoulders," Mike admitted in a sudden surge of openness.

Jonas regarded him with a calm gaze without judgment. "As a program leader, you need to prepare your program and your organization by building up that muscle for key decision making. The reason why I say this is that the majority of the delays to large-scale transformational initiatives are a result of slow decision making and/or poor decision making. By delaying critical decisions, you are opening the door for delays to the delivery and increase the cost of your transformation effort."

"What do I do, Jonas? I don't want to mess this up." Mike couldn't believe he was being so transparent with Jonas about his inner misgivings.

Jonas looked at him and nodded slightly. "You know, Mike, I work with a lot of people who are too proud to admit when they feel overwhelmed or that they're struggling. Because they don't try to get help, their projects get pushed toward overage and failure. I really respect that you'd ask me for help—after all, it's what I'm here for."

Mike smiled back weakly. "I just don't want to make *bad* decisions, Jonas. Too much is riding on this."

"So, one has to ask, with good critical success factors in place, and assuming that you have good processes in place, what is it that causes bad decisions to be made?"

"I don't know," Mike replied. "Not enough information? Insufficient training? Poor leadership?"

Jonas nodded soberly. "All good ideas. According to a good friend and colleague of mine who's done this as long as I have,[12] it comes down to three primary areas that can cause bad decisions. A lack of situational awareness, unchecked influence of cognitive biases, and a flawed decision lifecycle."

"So, what do you mean by a lack of situational awareness?" Mike asked.

Jonas replied, "Lack of situational awareness closely aligns with experience, but it is not the experience of making decisions. It's the experience of framing the problem to make the best decision. It is the ability to analyze all of the factors that contribute to a decision and the outcomes that are affected by a major decision."

"So, what happens without that experience?"

"An analogy I like to use is that of a mountain climber," Jonas told him. "Have you ever heard of the phrase, 'summit fever?'"

Mike shook his head no.

"It's when a mountain climber gets really close to the summit of a mountain. However, maybe their oxygen is running low, or a major storm is on the horizon. They have spent months or years of training for this moment, and they are so close to the top that they literally put their life at risk to reach the top of the mountain."

---

12   John Belden, Project Execution Advisory Services Practice Leader, Upper Edge

"Olay. So, they're so eager to get to the top that they take unnecessary risks?"

Jonas answered, "Think of a project or program that you have been on where the drive to complete on time was so hard that decisions were made to go live without taking into consideration the impacts to complete software testing or operational readiness. It's the ability to frame those perspectives outside your primary point of view that allows you to make fair and balanced decisions."

Mike had a sudden sinking feeling in his stomach that had nothing to do with the Mexican food. Too driven? That sounded a little too close to home.

"Sometimes, people have unchecked cognitive biases. A cognitive bias is a type of error in thinking that occurs when people are processing and interpreting information in the world around them. Some of these biases are related to the way you remember events of your past, which in turn can lead to biased thinking and decision-making. Other cognitive biases might be related to problems with attention. Since attention is a limited resource, people have to be selective about what they pay attention to in the world around them. Because of this, subtle biases can creep in and influence the way you see and think about the world. In the end, cognitive biases are often a result of your brain's attempt to simplify information processing. They are rules of thumb that help you make sense of the world and reach decisions with relative speed. Most of the time these 'shortcuts' serve us well, but on certain occasions, these biases can play a negative role in influencing our decision making. People who do this type of research for a living have identified 188 different cognitive biases."

"That's a lot," Mike said, trying to lighten the feeling he was under.

"Anchoring effect bias is a big one. This is where we, as humans, have the tendency to rely on the first number we see hear and anchor all future decisions on that number. A good example is a budget number or program scope. Once you hear that number, you mentally force yourself to stay within that frame for the duration of the program.

"Another cognitive bias is called the sunk cost bias, and this is the tendency of throwing good money after bad. A good example of this is when a program comes up with a good, lower-cost alternative to solving a problem, but the program manager does not pull the trigger because of the investment made in solving that problem to date and the hardship it would cause in throwaway work and possible financial write-offs.

"A third cognitive bias (and I will stop at three) is the expert bias. This is the tendency to make decisions based on perceived expertise. A good hypothetical example of this would be using Microsoft to be your system integrator for your Microsoft Dynamics implementation because Microsoft built the product. This is not a slam to Microsoft Consulting Services, as I have not worked with them in the past and have no base for opinion, it is only to demonstrate one's possible bias that just because a company builds product well it does not necessarily mean they know how to implement it well.

"The key point to make here is that you need to be as objective as possible, and you need to check for these cognitive biases in your personal decision making."

"You know, now that you mention this, Jonas," Mike said, "I have had a few people come up to me from senior leadership and bring up figures that were originally discussed by some of our vendors during the oral presentations—completely neglecting the follow-up conversations we had around the internal reality check we did on those figures, the risk budgets we put together, and the subsequent budget numbers I thought we all agreed on. At least I can now put a name to what I was experiencing during these conversations."

"Based on my initial look at your management dashboard figures, you may have a flawed decision-making lifecycle," Jonas told him. "This usually goes hand-in-hand with the very complex decisions that your program needs to have made to deliver successfully. Because these types of decisions are complex, that often means that they are integrated, and with integrated decisions, the number of stakeholders to engage in the decision-making process usually grows. And when the number of stakeholders grows, it usually means more frequent iterations and conversations surrounding the decisions, which usually means delays to the decision that actually has to be made. Another point that exacerbates this process is the lack of data or incorrect data. Each new stakeholder brings a different perspective to the table and may require different data to help in their decision-making process. This even further complicates the process and extends the lifecycle of the decision—all reflecting in delays to your program."

With the food cleared away, the two now just sat with their drinks in the increasingly empty Mexican restaurant, deep in conversation. Mike had never been so vulnerable with a colleague before, but Jonas' respectful, helpful attitude had drawn some of his biggest misgivings out of him.

"But what do I do about this flawed decision-making process that you are seeing from our dashboards, Jonas?" Mike grunted. "How do I *fix* it?"

"You're doing it right now," Jonas countered.

"Doing what? Eating Mexican?"

"No!" Jonas said, barking a laugh. "Leading the transformation. Talking to me. Learning processes. How do you think I learned how to do this?"

"I—I don't know."

"One decision at a time, Mike. Let's see if we can put some processes in place and provide you some leading practices to help improve your probability for successful decision making. It has a lot of similarities to our issue management process. I would call them very close cousins in our overall program governance strategy. The stages in our key decision process are identifying the key decisions to be made, evaluating the key decisions to be made—if necessary—escalating the key decision, finalizing the key decision, and monitoring the key decision process."

"Didn't we just have this conversation over salsa and chips?" Mike told him. Jonas chuckled, "Like I said, they're close cousins.

"The first stage of the key decision process is identification. We're trying to document all of the key decisions that need to be made for our program. Anyone on the program can identify a needed key decision. As part of a standard process, a key decision owner should be identified—if not to make the key decision, then to be the facilitator and influencer for the final decision. This means that this person should be a relatively senior person within your program or organization."

Jonas told him, "Once a key decision is initially logged, it should go through the evaluation process. Some key decisions may take time to close. For those longer-horizon decisions, you may want to collect them and perform a preliminary evaluation as a group and build out a decision dependency road map. This way, you can see how these key decisions will impact one another and how the effects of one decision can have on other decisions down the road. It will also provide you a high-level timeline as to when these key decisions need to be finalized.

"During the heads-down time of the evaluation process, the individual key decision is reviewed and analyzed for potential solutions. One key component during the evaluation process is identifying which deliverables across which projects will be impacted by this key decision and if any of those deliverables are on the program's critical path. The leading practice to use here is if this key decision is impacting a deliverable that is on or near the program's critical path, it needs to be dealt with and resolved *immediately* because that key decision is causing a day-for-day slip in the delivery of the overall program, essentially putting your overall program at risk."

"So, what do you do about it?"

Jonas answered, "The rule of thumb in this situation is to drop everything you are doing and get the right people in a room to resolve this key decision immediately. If the decision cannot be made by an individual or small group, then it needs to be escalated to a higher group for decision making."

"Up the escalators again, eh?" Mike quipped, thinking of Jonas' earlier joke and hoping *he* wasn't the guy who thought you had to go to the mall to escalate.

"Key decisions that cannot be resolved or requires a higher authority resolution are escalated to the appropriate level within your program. As part of the evaluation process, several alternatives should be documented and the recommended resolution provided. It provides context to a higher-level decision body that may not be as familiar with the issue or its context to the program.

"Similar to our issue resolution process, we should have due dates on these key decisions with an allowable grace period before the recommended decision becomes the final decision. This can get a little tricky depending on the significance and audience that needs to make the decision, so use your best judgment here.

"Once the recommended resolution is provided, the current owner will document it and provide additional comments as appropriate and then reassign the decision to the higher authority for the final resolution, or if the decision is already in the hands of the higher authority move directly into the final resolution stage."

"You're right," Mike noted, "this is pretty similar. So, then you finalize the decision? How does that work?"

"As part of the finalize key decision phase, the individual or group provides the action plan and resolution for the key decision. As part of the action plan, there should be a mini-communication plan on who needs to be informed about this key decision. Once the key decision action plan is complete, and the key decision is documented by the key decision owner, the key decision originator (along with all of the stakeholders discussed in the action plan) are informed of the final decision. At that point, the key decision originator can close out the key decision."

"Then, we track it?" Mike asked.

Jonas nodded. "The last stage in key decision management is key decision tracking. During this stage, the project managers will ensure that the overall key decision process is being executed properly within their team and that documentation of the key decision generated from their team follows your program standards. Through these good documentation practices, we will be able to quickly comply with any program audit requests. Additionally, your project managers will perform analysis on the key decisions associated with their project areas and provide any necessary escalations."

"Okay," Mike said. "Carlos told me that AMIGO has a really cool feature that allows it send out communications about key decisions to all resources who are responsible for deliverables associated with the same domain as the key decision, correct?"

"That is correct. This is part of AMIGO's AI messaging functionality that will search through its network map and identify all of the people who are responsible for deliverables associated to a given object, as well as the project managers associated to projects with that object. And then automatically inform them that a key decision has been made that may have an impact on their body of work. This functionality greatly improves the lines of communication and significantly reduces the risk of 'gotchas' when you get to systems integration testing."

"That is pretty awesome, I must say," Mike replied while sipping on his virgin margarita.

Jonas continued, "Getting back to the overall process, your program leadership will review key decisions on at least a weekly basis and should be measuring the velocity at which key decisions are being made. Again, those key decisions that are impacting the program's critical path are dealt with immediately. Do not wait until the next meeting to discuss them. Schedule an emergency meeting with all the appropriate responsible, accountable, and consulted resources for the key decision and resolve it immediately. On certain programs, we would refer to these as SWAT team meetings—because things were so critical that you had to bring in the key players and decision-makers to reduce the threat to the program like a SWAT team would in a crisis situation. So that's the key decision management process."

Jonas paused for a moment to take a drink of his virgin mojito, or, as the restaurant called it, "vojito," and continued on. "Do you want my seven keys to quality decision making?"

Mike smiled. "Definitely. Lay them on me."

"When you've got your list of key decisions," Jonas told him, "you should be in good shape to try out your new key decision process and key decision teams and start flexing those decision-making muscles.

"Start testing your *process*. Does your process hold up? Are there any cracks or flaws in the hand-offs amongst the stages? Are the proper governance and controls in place?

"Start testing your *teams*. Do they hold up? Are they strong enough to make the decisions? Do they have the authority to make those decisions stick and be successful?"

"What if they don't?"

"This is when you need to have some serious conversations with your boss, Charles, to see what can be done to beef up aspects of the key decision boards and steerco to help drive these decisions."

"All right, I'll consider that," Mike replied.

Jonas continued, "The next thing you want to do is take those open decisions and lay out the sequence and dependencies in which they need to be made. This will help lay out your decision-making critical path. The decisions to be made on this path should be well in front of the completion of work packages that need those decisions that are on your program's critical chain."

"So, you're getting out ahead of it," Mike noted.

"Right. But not just with these decisions. My next recommendation is to bake these decisions into your training program. Go into detail as to why the decisions that were made were actually made. Give the users the thought processes and what was considered in the process.

"What this will do is give your power users a better appreciation for what it took to get to this point of the program and an appreciation for the thought that went into the decision itself. When your power users are onboard and armed with this intelligence of what the program had to go through and the decisions that needed to be made, they will be able to explain the same to their constituents and be a great conduit for your overall change management.

"The next tip is to elevate your decision-making metrics to the top of your program management dashboard. The same principles apply from the issue management process I mentioned earlier. You see, the velocity of issue resolution and decision-making ability is a good indicator and predictor of on-time delivery of your digital transformation. Keep your velocity high, and your probability of delivering on-time increases."

"I like the sound of that."

"I bet you do," Jonas replied, smiling. "Additionally, build dependencies on the project and deliverables that need that key decision. This, along with the decision-making dependency we discussed earlier, will be good indicators to determine just how fast and at what velocity your key decisions need to be made."

Mike frowned as he thought. "Except not all decisions are equal, like we talked about before. If politics get into the mix..."

"That's right, and that's why decision vetting and challenge sessions are important. That's usually used for those very complex and very integrated types of decisions that need to be made on your program. Although we are always worried about velocity from a program delivery point of view, don't forget what I told you about summit fever and making impulsive decisions without situational awareness."

"I haven't. It hit too close to home," Mike admitted.

"Well, this is why we have this step—to really vet out those critical complex decisions. For these decisions, you want to have multiple stakeholders with multiple lenses looking at the problem from different angles. Then, through very facilitated working sessions, work that group to come to a decision that all can be comfortable with or at least support.

"This approach serves so many purposes: It is a bridge to executive alignment and teamwork. It also demonstrates that though not everyone will get their way, they can work together for the betterment of the organization, support the decision, and cascade that support down their lines of business. When brought into the training materials as we described before, it becomes a great agent for change and adoption."

"So, this helps guard against summit fever?" Mike asked.

"It does. It's like a check and balance system."

Mike finished his drink. "Anything else?"

Jonas thought for a moment. "The last recommendation I have is to develop a comprehensive key decision document or template. This document should outline what's required for the key decision as well as all of the inputs necessary to make the key decision, such as system integrator inputs, expectations from both internal and external subject matter experts as well as their inputs, the documentation of any cognitive biases that may come into play, as well as mitigation strategies for those cognitive biases. And yes, before you ask, this has already been done for you in AMIGO."

Jonas took a final drink, and then the two men stood up together. The sinking, tight feeling Mike had felt earlier in the day—and again when Jonas had mentioned summit fever—had eased. Once again, Jonas' information had answered some of his most pressing concerns.

Mike had a renewed vigor in his step as he mentally formulated his plan of action to get his project leaders, peers, and executive team focused on resolving the critical issues and making the key decisions that were slowing down the progress on the program.

CHAPTER 17

Scope and Change Control

Mike and Nancy were adjusting to a new normal now that cancer was in their lives. For Nancy, that meant dealing with the reality of chemo treatments, and Mike couldn't decide whether to think of it as a horror or a miracle. Maybe it was partly both.

Nancy's schedule revolved around these treatments. Her first four were doxorubicin, which was the color of a rich, red house paint and so toxic the nurses administering it had to wear outfits fit for a hazmat crew. The seven or so hour-long treatments involved being hooked to an IV most of that time and getting a cocktail of drugs designed to reduce the chance of having a serious allergic reaction. The IV included both steroids and Benadryl, which seemed to have opposing effects. The steroids made her want to run around the room; the Benadryl made her want to go to sleep. She spent most of the time hooked to the IV torn between these two states.

The treatments would knock her flat for a couple of days, so at first, that cycle dominated their lives. However, after the doxorubicin treatments came a "milder" chemo that most people tolerated better. She was supposed to have these once a week, but Nancy wasn't most people, so her body responded poorly to the new drug, and she ended up traveling back to the hospital three to five days a week for immune-boosting shots designed to get her blood counts—mostly red and white blood cells and platelets—back to the levels they needed to be so she could have another treatment.

Nancy's world ended up revolving around this treatment schedule, and therefore so did the kids—and so did Mike. As a result, both Mike and Nancy knew they would need extended help so they asked Nancy's mom, Anna, if she could move in with them for the long haul.

Anna helped Nancy through the days after chemo treatments, as well as giving the kids rides to their activities on occassion, but Mike also found himself pulled away from work for an hour or so to get somebody somewhere, only to have to come back and make up the time long after "quitting time."

Neighbors and friends brought meals for which the family was incredibly grateful. Mike worked too much and did what he could, and the incredible chaos settled into an uncomfortable, if somewhat predictable, rhythm. It became their new normal.

In the transformation program, they were getting close to the end of the design of the new digital product. Mike, Jonas, and Carlos were taking a working lunch at Fat Guy's, Mike's favorite burger place.

Mike took a big bite of his poison of choice, a Signature Heartstopper. He hadn't been able to eat most of the day, his stomach still tied in knots after Nancy's morning appointment. Now it was finally unclenched, and he was hungry.

Jonas was eating more slowly. "You're right," he said around a mouth full. "This is one of the best burgers I've ever had."

Mike scooped up some fries and dunked them in ketchup. "So, we were going to talk about scope management over lunch, right?"

Carlos nodded back to him, finished chewing, and said, "Yep, let's get to it. So, you've done the first part by defining the overall scope of your program. You collected the requirements, you performed a scope definition, and you took that scope definition and put it into a work breakdown structure and then verified that scope. Then you went and built out your high-level program plan with all of your projects, methodologies, deliverables, work packages, estimated efforts, dependencies, and roles, RACI, and you developed an estimated timeline for this effort. Then you sat down with your leadership as well as mine and Covice's leadership and did a final walkthrough to verify the scope, effort, timelines, and any key assumptions, built the appropriate statements of work, and had everyone signoff, right?"

Mike nodded. "You've summed up my first few months on this program in thirty seconds, quite impressive, sir." Jonas and Carlos smiled at Mike's retort.

"Okay. So, you have these agreements now, and this becomes your approved statement of work, as well as the legal or commercial statement of work for your consultants, in particular your commercial relationships with Gley & Stratton and Covice. After those agreements were signed, you were ready to start the delivery of your new digital transformation initiative. And now your teams are having their workshops and envisioning and designing what this digital product will look like when it is all said and done, and that is when you started experiencing some changes to what you thought was going to be your reality, correct?" Jonas asked.

"Change—the one universal constant," Mike muttered.

"That and death," Carlos jumped in.

"And taxes," Jonas added. Mike didn't comment on this, but he felt that his stomach clenched up again when Carlos said, "death." Suddenly, the remainder of his fries didn't look very appealing.

Oblivious to what was going on in Mike's mind, Carlos said, "Change, for all intent and purposes, is inevitable in your program. Unless you are installing an out-of-the-box, plug and play, no changes allowed cloud solution, like Office 365, you are most likely going to have some changes. How you control and manage those changes is what's most important."

Mike didn't find something to say, but he knew changes were bound to happen. "So, how to do we do that?" he asked.

Jonas told him, "Your program needs to have a rigorous and disciplined change control process. Without it, you are going to be one of those statistics of failed IT-enabled transformation initiatives. The process has five steps: identification, impact assessment, approval, implement, and monitor and control."

"Hold on," Mike said, getting out his phone to take notes.[13]

When he had it, Jonas went on—from memory. "When you get the first whiff of a change coming about, you are going to want to identify that change. As a rule, anyone on the team can identify and document the initial change request. However, for this change to have legs and get through the change control process, it is going to need a sponsor. That sponsor should be someone with influence in your program who can properly represent and defend the need for this change request.

"It is really good at this time to start getting your ducks in a row and start building the benefits case for the requested change. You see, there is a program cost in the next step of the process, the impact assessment. Because you are going to have to take people off of already pre-defined deliverables and work packages and ask them to work on something that is not part of their resource capacity. Right there, you are putting work packages and timelines at risk. So if you want to have any chance of getting your identified change through to the next step, you're going to have to have a pretty compelling reason; otherwise, your change review board (at least a good one) will not make the investment in the impact assessment."

"That makes sense," Mike commented. "You hope they do a good job and don't just approve any old thing. I don't want scope creep."

Jonas replied, "When we think of scope and scope creep, we are usually looking at it from the point of view of adding scope. But there are those occasions where the needle goes the other way. When we built our original plan and estimates, it was with the best intentions and with the best knowledge that we had at that time. However, things change—life changes—and sometimes our estimates are off."

You have no idea how much life changes, Mike thought to himself.

Carlos added, "What if we had planned to build fifty integrations, but it turns out that only forty-five integrations are necessary? In these situations, you still want to put this change through our scope management process as a descoping change request."

"I've never thought about that side of it. How do you handle that?"

----

13 For more information, please go to www.platinumpmo.com/thetransformationbook

"We follow the same process, but our benefits case will be more geared towards the program savings instead of its impact on the organizational benefit," Jonas answered.

"Another concept is 'scope swap' or trading scope," Jonas went on. "Using the same scenario we just described, we may determine that we no longer need those five integrations, but to descope those five integrations, we need to add three more data conversion objects. This becomes a little more complicated change request, but it's still achievable with our process.

"The rule of thumb that I would use for a trading scope change request is to only perform these types of change requests when there is *true* integration quid pro quo, meaning that you can't descope unless you add scope, or vice versa. If there is no true integration, my suggestion would be to treat them as two separate changes—one for descoping and another for scope addition—and let the change review board decide their fates independently."

"So, they can stand on their own merits," Mike added, thinking out loud.

"Right," Jonas agreed. "Assuming your change review board approves the initial request, your change request moves to the next stage, which is the impact assessment. This can be a pretty time-consuming effort depending on the complexity of the change and the impact it may have on one or many projects within your digital transformation program. Your change review board must remain diligent in approving this initial request and not take this responsibility lightly, because once they do, they are making an unplanned investment into the program. They are essentially authorizing a request to pull one or more people off of their planned work to perform the impact assessment for a potentially considerable amount of time."

"The impact assessment owner must do their due diligence to identify all the aspects of the program that can be impacted by this change request. As part of this analysis, the impact assessment owner will essentially go through all the levers of scope that were used to define the program and analyze where the impacts might be.

"It is important that the impact assessment owner provide high-level estimates of impact for each project or project deliverable that will need to be changed as a result of this change request so that the change review board has a full understanding of the impact.

"While this work is going on, the change request sponsor can continue to do their due diligence on the supporting business case—further quantifying the revenue-generating capabilities, cost reduction capabilities, or risk avoid components that this change will have to the business to further defend the merits of this change request and position it for development approval."

"If the juice is worth the squeeze," Mike commented. He'd heard Jonas say it before, and he could tell the older man liked hearing it back from him.

"Indeed. At this stage, your change review board should be taking a hard look at the benefits case for the change and the associated impact and risks this change may have on your overall program. As part of their analysis, they will need to assess the accuracy of the estimates, the number of integration impacts associated to the change, the current state of the program (are they behind or ahead of schedule?), the available capacity across the changes to take on the additional work, as well as the reserve funds available to pay for the additional work.

"When they factor these, and whatever other factors or standards have been established by this governance board, they will need to ask themselves if the benefits of the change outweigh the cost and potential implementation to the program. If the answer is yes, you move on to the development stage."

Mike held up a hand, got up, and refilled his drink. His mind was swirling with Jonas's download of scope control, and when he sat back down, he asked, "At this stage, how do you know what kind of impact this change will have on the implementation timeline?"

Jonas replied, "That is a great question," looking at Carlos as though to say, 'See, I told you he asks good questions.' He went on, "This is the type of question you should be asking your change sponsor and change review board every time one of these high-impacting changes come up. You see, the sponsor is looking at the change as a piece of functionality that is going to help his business, the change review board is looking at the change primarily from a dollars and cents and value perspective, but we need someone looking at it from an integration and implementation impact. In other words, can we add this scope and resource its development without compromising our implementation timelines? This is where you will need to look at your resource capacity, maybe simulate the change and run a critical chain analysis and determine if you have enough capacity to not impact your timeline and ask if you need to bring on additional resources to not impact the timeline."

"That's great information, Jonas. I will be sure to make those challenges," Mike replied.

Jonas continued, "So, now that you have done that prep work, as part of the approval stage, the change request has been funded, and a development manager has been assigned. As part of the preparation, the development manager will formally go through the impact assessments and the requirements of the change and build out all of that prep work that has been established as part of the process so far into their detailed plan. Depending on the thoroughness of the impact assessment, this can be an easy or difficult task. The development manager will update their project plans to account for the additional work and get the work going into their planned workstreams.

"Now, here is where it can get a little tricky on what you do with this change request next. It all really depends on where you are in the lifecycle of your program. If you are in the initial development stage or earlier of your program, you will just take on this work as part of what you need to do for preparation for system or integration test. If you are already in a system or integration test cycle and the challenge is to get this change in as soon as possible, you would then submit this change request to the change review board for final review and release to test environment approval. If you are already in production, and this is an urgent change request to your production environment, you would now be asking to have it approved for your quality environment and then hopefully for your production environment.

"As part of this stage, the change review board has the final disposition on if, where, and when this change request should be deployed."

After a moment, Jonas added, "The monitor and control process is where all of your process controls, governance, and reporting occurs. I highly recommend that you have an automated control system to handle this process." He shot Carlos a meaningful gaze. He was looking at his phone and almost missed it, putting it on the table hurriedly. "On most programs, there are millions of dollars at stake for these change control processes. Running your process controls and reports on spreadsheets, emails, and PowerPoints is not a good way to govern this sum of money."

"Yeah, no joke," Carlos said dryly. "If only there were some software out in the marketplace that could handle this," Carlos said sheepishly while stroking his goatee.

Tips for Controlling Scope

Jonas took a drink, and then continued, "There was a recent study I read that said that 75 percent of IT professionals think that their project is doomed from the start. Do you know why?"

"I can guess."

"Regularly changing project requirements leads to scope creep, which ultimately creates a gap between your business goals and project objectives. Ask any program manager—they will all tell you that scope creep is their worst nightmare."

"No one really likes scope creep," Carlos added.

"So, what do you do about it?" Mike asked. "I know you've got some things that've worked."

Jonas had a twinkle in his eye as he replied with false modesty, "Yeah, I've got a few tips I can share. But it'll cost you."

Mike laughed. "Cost me? We're already paying you pretty well!"

Jonas was grinning as he nodded over to the counter. "It's not much—I think we should stay for milkshakes. One is calling my name, I think."

"I think we can handle that," Mike said, continuing to laugh. He was pretty full, but a milkshake did sound pretty good. He looked at Carlos, who held up his hand in a shrug, adding he could go for one too.

A few minutes later, cold, chocolatey goodness flowing down his throat, and Mike sat back down. Jonas took a long drink and then began. "Sounds simple, but the first step is to define the scope of the project in detail. By going through the levers of scope and developing your deliverables and subsequent work packages, you'll have a firm handle on the boundaries surrounding your program.

"A clearly defined scope of work is an important part of setting expectations at the beginning of a project. It will be much easier to identify and manage scope creep by documenting the details of your project before you *start* work."

"Which is why we're talking about this now."

"Precisely." Jonas sucked on his straw, having to work for it because the shake was thick and rich. "So, I suggest you discuss deliverables, timelines, milestones, duties, and responsibilities for both you and your vendors. Collaborate to outline a clear plan of action that will help you both meet the project goal. As you gather a list of requirements, be sure to speak with all stakeholders involved to ensure you don't overlook anything.

"Make sure you understand what is—and isn't—in scope. Don't just send a document outlining the deliverables—speak to them and walk your vendors through it properly. Be transparent: ask questions such as, 'Are you clear on what this deliverable is and what you'll get?' Then create a scope management plan in your project planning phase."

"How big does it need to be?"

"It doesn't have to be a fifty-page document. You just need to know how you will manage scope changes and make sure your sponsor agrees with the process," Carlos said with his mouth around his straw.

"I've seen a lot of scope change requests that explain the benefits of the change," Jonas said. "When you take this to the sponsor, the sponsor will very likely say yes, since all they see is the benefits. They don't see the impact on the project. As we discussed a little while ago, it is usually the case that scope changes require more work—and this can lead to an impact on schedule and budget. But don't stop there. Often, scope changes will increase project *risk*. They may have staffing implications. They may impact vendors (procurements). The key is to identify the total *impact* of your project on all elements of project management.

"By establishing a rigorous change control process and establishing a strong governing change review board, you already have half the battle won. Now all you need to do is the benefits and impact due diligence to combat scope creep."

Combatting Scope Creep

"So, how granular should we get with our scope management? Every day, there is going to be 'change' at some level. At what level do we actually manage scope change?"

"Great question," Carlos chimed in. "Often, the project manager and project team don't recognize when a change has occurred. That's a sign of scope creep. These are small, incremental changes that we either do not recognize as scope changes, or we choose to ignore them because they're small. This is the proverbial death by a thousand paper cuts."

"All scope changes should be recognized and taken through your scope management process. Small changes may have their own simple process for evaluation and approval, but all of the changes need to be managed," Jonas added.

"AMIGO has great change control process built into its platform," Carlos said. "Not only does AMIGO do a great job at tracking your changes, but it has that AI capability I was telling you about earlier that will send micro communications to every resource who has a direct or indirect association with a given change request."

Jonas added, "I have been on so many projects where change requests are discussed, reviewed, and approved in a vacuum. And after the change was implemented, three or four teams start screaming, 'What the hell just happened?' because no one informed them of the change and the impact it would have on the work they were doing."

Carlos said, "With AMIGO, the software is intelligent enough to understand the impact points and will send messages to those resources working on tangential parts of the program that may be impacted by this change and give them a heads up about what's going on. It's a really powerful feature."

Mike acknowledged, "Yeah, the more I am learning about AMIGO, the more I like it. I am glad we are using it and that Gley & Stratton has embedded the platform into their delivery services."

Jonas continued on, "Every time you change deliverables, boundaries, or requirements, make sure that you document the change and then review its impact. Each change does not need a separate scope change form, but all changes should be documented in your change log. Then you will be sure that your initial scope, plus your scope change log, will be reflected in the final deliverables. If you make verbal scope changes without documenting them, there will be a gap between the agreed scope and your final solution that may be difficult to explain."

"AMIGO can help with that," Carlos added.

"You wouldn't think small changes would have a big effect, but I guess they can all add up," Mike mused.

"Right, but remember, these changes don't happen in a vacuum. They can impact the entire program. For example, if a designer decides to include some functionality on a site without discussing it with the developer, who knows what this could do to your overall scope, without any investigation?" Jonas said.

He went on, "Make sure you set your team up from the beginning of a project to work together and understand each other's decisions. When someone raises a query or issue with you directly, share it with everyone if there's a bigger decision to be made. Get people working together to define and find solutions to problems. Make sure everyone is regularly in contact (whether face-to-face or remotely). Most successful projects are enabled by teams that work well together and clearly communicate and collaborate.

"To prevent this situation, you should establish two-way communications and communicate regularly with your vendors. A communication gap between clients and project managers usually leads to scope creep, which could push your project towards failure."

"Good two-way communication," Carlos said, taking a drink. "Isn't that what we're doing?"

"Failure is not an option," Mike muttered. It was the mantra he'd been repeating to himself for weeks—now for the transformation and with their cancer battle.

"This is why it is so essential to have a good, thorough scope of work," Jonas explained. "You're going to have change requests for your vendors, and you need to both be able to come back to the original scope. Additional change orders will either add on the requested work at an additional expense, or you can proceed with the agreed-upon scope of work.

"When you are up against scope creep or managing a dynamic project, effective change management is crucial for success. Managing changes to the original scope of work is critical to keeping projects under control."

Mike nodded. "I can see that it's important to use change control forms to analyze the impact that the changes might have on time, cost, and essentiality."

Jonas told him, "Program managers are fully responsible for not only tracking these changes but also testing them before implementation. Although these activities can take a lot of time, they can reap the rewards when it comes to resolving scope creep issues. If they do their job, you will be able to properly assess the cost/benefit of the change and have a full understanding of the impact this change will have on your program with fully vetted alternatives to choose from."

"What if they just need more time?" Mike asked. "Maybe we didn't allocate enough when we were planning?"

Carlos added, "This is an age-old issue. Estimation is very difficult to get right. It's a challenge for a vendor to be accurate at the beginning of a project when there are many unknowns. Certain things may not get accounted for, and they end up tied to this extra scope to be able to deliver your overall project."

"Right," Mike agreed. "How can they accurately estimate how many bugs will be raised, how long they will take to fix, and what impact this will have?"

"Well, a couple of things come to mind," Jonas replied. "First, they need to involve their whole team in estimation upfront. Don't work in a silo and make guesses. They need to ensure they've compared business requirements to user requirements before estimating. This approach will also help with the team's buy-in to the whole program or project as they were engaged in setting up these estimates; they will own its delivery.

"We can also help mitigate this old problem by using the critical chain technique. Through statistical modeling, we can estimate a percentage of the overall work to be part of our contingency buckets for those work packages that go over the initially estimated forecast. Remember, statistically speaking, fifty percent of the time, things will get delivered under budget and fifty percent of the time, things will be delivered over budget. Use your buffer management technique to manage these ebbs and flows."

"Scope creep generally applies to projects with a fixed scope, right?" Mike mused. "What if you are using an agile methodology?"

"Well, agile embraces change—and frankly, so should you. If you're working within different processes or methodologies change should not be seen as the enemy," Carlos said.

"As one of the core principles of agile states," Jonas said, "'*Welcome changing requirements, even late in development. Agile processes harness change for the customer's competitive advantage.*' If you're working according to scrum methodology, for example, when a new requirement comes in, pull it into the sprint planning meeting and get it in the backlog. Prioritize it with the product owner and team, and if it does go into the sprint, something else will be deprioritized instead. Because details aren't determined at the beginning of the project, change can be incorporated. Stories can be swapped quite easily for other stories if they require the same effort.

"The point of agile is to iterate, which means designing, building, testing, learning, and then repeating the cycle. Remember, change is what leads to the best possible product in the time you have."

"So, what actually counts as scope creep in an agile project?" Mike asked.

Carlos answered, "Since you should have the ability to change scope quite easily without throwing the whole project to the lions, scope creep in agile doesn't really affect you until later down the line."

"Scope creep could come into play if your product owner doesn't deprioritize features or tasks when pulling something in," Jonas added. "For instance, they may want to add something into the current cycle without removing something else. Also, they might not weigh the effort needed between the new task and the deprioritized one, which could result in trying to cram extra effort into an already planned cycle that's too tight.

"The other thing that bites product owners using the agile method in the butt is that when they are making decisions of what is going to be in and out of their individual product, they don't consider the implications to the other integrated products around them. This is where product owner communications is paramount.

"Also, make sure that, for any new features entering the backlog, you're effectively breaking these down into stories and understanding the effort against them so that you can prioritize accordingly. If you have a product owner who understands this process, scope creep will be much less of a threat. In general, it's a lot easier to mitigate scope creep in an agile project, precisely because change is encouraged and factored into the structure of the methodology itself.

"As the product owner, you have to mindful of your program's time and budget constraints. Though you are handling stories, functions, and features at your product level, you have to understand the impacts this may have on the overall program. Your product owner needs to have the discipline to keep the balanced scorecard of changes out and changes in, especially when additional time or money is involved. In the event a particular project or product cannot deliver the essentials needed for the overall program to meet its timeline and budget, you will have to go through your change control process. Your product owner will be your change request sponsor and will need to work with the change review board to get these additions added to the overall program budget and/or timeline."

"So, if we're using agile, it doesn't sound like it's as big a deal," Mike commented.

Jonas looked at him somewhat crossly. "One of the biggest reasons why scope creep negatively affects projects is because project managers take it lightly and ignore it. Spending the time upfront to lay the groundwork and clearly define the scope will help keep the project on track.

"When you inevitably make out-of-scope requests, don't be shy about telling them that you'll add their request to 'Phase 2' of the project, which will have its own scope and cost. To prevent scope creep or manage it efficiently, you will have to push aggressively to eliminate it and follow a proactive approach instead of a laid-back one."

"Taking change lightly doesn't do anyone any favors," Carlos added, looking at Jonas. "But one of the best features of AMIGO is that these change requests will be clearly processed and not get lost in the cracks."

Mike nodded, checking his watch. They needed to get back. "This was a great lunch, guys. I really appreciate your insights, and I'm sure I will be asking for your opinions on the multitude of change requests that are and will continue to come down the pike throughout this implementation."

They stood up, threw away their now empty milkshake cups, and headed out of the restaurant. After all they'd consumed, Mike felt like they might need to roll him out, but he also had a much clearer understanding of scope and change control. He would be sure to take scope creep serious and not let it sneak up on them, and it sounded like AMIGO would make it all easier.

CHAPTER 18

Slipping

Eleven months had passed since Mike became the program director for Extron's digital transformation initiative. Nancy had gone through a great deal of treatment for breast cancer, and Mike had been there for her as much as he could along the way. The "new normal" in the Bennett household was still pretty chaotic.

Though he loved his mother-in-law, Mike felt like his home was under a new set of rules with Anna permanently underfoot, which—on occasion—would cause some serious tension. Plus, there was the added stress of Gabbi's drug counseling sessions and school meetings with teachers for Donny alongside visits with a therapist to evaluate his quarterly performance against his IEP (individualized education program) for his autism. Then there was the "special session" MJ's teacher wanted to have to discuss his growing outbursts and disruptions during class time. Nancy's treatment schedule was also keeping Mike busy, as was work's increasing demands.

Mike wasn't sleeping much, drank too much coffee, and was tempted to schedule a visit to the doctor for a bottle of Xanax.

He hadn't been able to make many of Nancy's appointments lately, but today he'd been able to arrange his schedule so he could be there at her final chemotherapy treatment. It was a major milestone; she'd gone through treatments with two different drugs, and the second one had been very hard on her. While others said they found it easier than the so-called "Red Devil" (the big gun they hit her with four times initially), the second med had knocked her blood's important indicators down so much that she hadn't always been able to have her treatment on schedule. Now—many shots designed to artificially stimulate red blood cells and other body processes later—she was hooked up for her final chemo.

Mike watched Nancy interact with nurses who had become friends during this difficult process—men and women she routinely encouraged as they struggled with their own lives. They smiled and chatted and joked around him like quick-moving birds. The fact never ceased to blow Mike's mind that Nancy had an attitude still focused on helping others while she was being intentionally poisoned to kill the cancer. How could she have such a great attitude while facing this horrible illness and its difficult treatment?

After the bag on the cart she was hooked to was done, one nurse Nancy seemed to like a lot, a young guy named Rodrigo, came over and carefully unhooked the IV line from the port that had been surgically implanted into Nancy's chest. Rod had an open face, and he often fell victim to Nancy's jokes that preyed on his naiveté, like when—while under the conflicting influence of both massive amounts of Benadryl and steroids—she had told him that the bruise marks on her arms were from shooting drugs. Today, Rod had a broad smile, and Mike could sense the anticipation in him and his wife as he deftly drew the massive gauge needle from Nancy's port. With a few swift moves, he had her bandaged up and ready to go.

Nancy looked at Mike, then to her mom, who was also there for this momentous day. She carefully stood up, Mike under her arm, and began making her way toward a big metal bell anchored to the wall of the hospital's infusion lab. With each step, it seemed like she grew steadier and steadier, like she was gaining steam and confidence as she walked.

All around the room, nurses—and to a lesser extent, patients—stopped and looked up. Some shouted encouragement, nodded, or cheered as she walked. Anna had her phone out, recording everything as Nancy grabbed the rope tied to the bell—and rang it loudly. Many people only gave a couple of pulls—*ding, ding*—but not Nancy. She grabbed that rope and pulled and pulled, banging out one powerful note after another and nearly pulling the bell off the wall!

Everyone who cared went nuts, cheering and shouting—including Nancy, who was half crying, half yelling at the top of her lungs. When Mike saw that she'd shaken the bell loose from its housing, he gently put his hand over hers, cutting it short perhaps by a few rings but hopefully keeping the big bell on the wall.

Mike was smiling along with everyone else and had even shouted a little as she walked up and started ringing, but somehow, he felt disconnected. Maybe it was because he'd been thinking about work and couldn't shift gears to the present, but maybe there was more to it. He wasn't sure, but his workload had been increasing and Anna had started replacing him at appointments, and he didn't like how that was making him feel. It was like he didn't quite belong, that he hadn't really earned this victory with Nancy, that he should've been there for her more.

He shelved the feelings, put on a happy face, and hugged his wife fiercely—but not too hard. A few minutes later, Mike pulled the car up to the chilly infusion lab so that Nancy could climb directly into the hot vehicle. Then the feelings of discomfort returned. He had to get her home and get back to work; there just wasn't time for melancholy when there was so much work to do.

Mike's feeling of disassociation—like he was there but not *fully*—lasted through his drive back to work and even as he entered the building and headed for his office. He plopped down into his chair for just a moment and shook his head as though that would clear it, but when that didn't help, he jumped up to get some coffee.

A few minutes later, he was numbly staring at some queries he'd run to look over some of the project's critical chain fever charts plus Jonas' seven keys to success. All he saw was yellow and red indicators, and he felt his stomach clenching.

Things had started to feel like they were coming unglued and that the master plan was not working.

Mike texted Jonas, asking to set up a meeting. It was late in the day—Nancy's appointments could last six or seven hours—so they set up a time to meet the following day. By the time Mike had wandered out of the office, he felt like he'd hardly gotten a thing done despite the fact it was nearly 8:00 p.m.

His mind wandered as he drove home, where he found the house quiet. Anna had taken the boys to their various after-school activities while Gabbi was hanging out with friends next door. He peeked into his bedroom to find Nancy sleeping. Her face was pale—she hadn't looked well for the last couple of months—and he could see how thin she'd become during the treatments. Something about the power of her personality disguised how sick she was from the chemo when she was in motion, but now, with her still, he could see it more clearly.

Everyone had already eaten something that Anna had whipped up. Mike found leftovers, cracked open a beer, and ate by himself with the TV on but volume low, closed captioning filling him in as SportsCenter gave him the rundown.

He didn't have much appetite, and his thoughts fell back to the reports he'd viewed before leaving work. He didn't feel like he was fully there for Nancy—didn't feel fully part of that world where she lived so much of her life—but as he thought about the reports, he didn't feel like he was doing a great job at work right now, either. It was slipping. He was losing it, and he was afraid he wouldn't be able to get it back under control.

The gnawing fear for Nancy's life that he had pushed deep back into the basement of his soul bubbled up with thoughts of her pale, drawn face—and then got all mixed up with the seemingly worsening state of affairs at work. Then he thought of the troubles with the kids, wondered how each was truly doing and how this cancer was impacting them and their situations. Then Mike berated himself for not knowing the answers or how to fix them.

The transformation project was eating his lunch. He didn't feel like he had a good handle on it right now after seeing the queries come back, but he didn't feel like he was doing his personal life justice, either. It was like there just wasn't enough Mike to go around.

After another few beers, he drifted off on the couch, where Nancy found him and put a blanket on him sometime in the night. In the den in the back of the house, he hadn't even heard Anna come home with the kids. Nancy didn't wake him; she knew he hadn't been sleeping well. She just kissed his head, said a prayer, and let Mike sleep his exhausted sleep.

CHAPTER 19

Recovery

Mike was leaning his head back on his office chair's headrest with his eyes closed, squeezing the bridge of his nose between his forefinger and thumb. He was manually trying to pinch the last of the headache out of his forehead, which sometimes worked—but only when combined with the two Excedrin Migraine, half a bottle of water, and an antacid tablet. He'd gotten to work early and had been looking over the queries he'd run, struggling to see the connections. The headache was not uncommon for him, but it probably wasn't made better by the beers and night on the couch. Then there was a knock at the door.

"Come on in," Mike said.

Jonas entered. He was his usual unruffled self with his traditional small smile. "You look stressed," he commented, grabbing a chair.

"Thanks, nice to see you, too," Mike shot back. He'd intended it to be funny, but it came out rougher than he'd meant. "Sorry. Yes, I'm stressed. Thanks for responding to my call last night. I was reviewing some of my program data before I left the office last night, and I was not liking what I was seeing. Many areas all across the program are slipping, and I'm trying to make sense of what the heck is going on, and I could use a second set of eyes on the data for some perspective."

"You know," Jonas said slowly, "every project has moments like this.

Things start to slide, and you've got to catch them."

"'Start to slide?'" Mike echoed. "They've slid, buddy—they're already in the toilet."

Jonas accepted Mike's acid without batting an eye. "I know you feel like that, but what you're seeing is pretty common."

"For failures."

"No," Jonas said back, a slight edge of correction in his voice, "for *transformations*. You think it's always smooth sailing for those who do it 'just right?'" He shook his head. "Mike, you're a smart guy, but no one is so smart that their project is going to go off without a hitch. Bumps in the road are part of it. It's how we address these challenges that's important for success or failure."

Mike didn't know what to say. He opened his mouth a few times, but then he closed it without replying.

"Let's take a look at the data and see if we can come up with some answers. Your order-to-cash is red and has been for a couple of weeks. What seems to be the problem?"

"I don't know, Jonas. I can't seem to figure it out, and neither can my OTC project manager. The team looks busy, the meter is running, but we are not moving anywhere."

"Have you looked at their issues log in detail lately? Why don't we pull it up and take a look?" Mike went into AMIGO and pulled up the issues logged and filtered it to focus on the open issues for the order-to-cash team. Jonas looked at the twenty-plus open issues on the screen. "Look at the 'days opened' field on this report. Some of these issues have been open for more than twenty days! My guess is that people on the OTC team are waiting for answers to these issues and no one is escalating and providing the answers. I would be sitting down with this team, and all of your project managers, for that matter, to talk about this because I bet it's happening on other teams, too.

"I'll bet if you open up these issues, you will not see many alternative solutions or a recommended solution to solve the issue. A good leading practice that will keep momentum going and improve your issue resolution velocity is to define alternatives and a recommendation for each issue that you can. This gives the assigned owner some thoughts from the team to aid in their decision. Also, set some standard guidelines with your PMs on when to escalate or go with the recommended solution."

"What do you recommend?" Mike asked.

"Start with a five-day rule. If the issue is not resolved on the fourth day, your PM will go to the issue owner and inform him or her that we are going forward with the recommended solution if we don't get your answer by tomorrow (the fifth day). This should increase your throughput and put those idle hands back to delivering value."

"Great suggestion, Jonas. Can we take a look at the integration team next? They have been red for four weeks now."

Jonas again started by looking at the issues log. "Nothing's jumping out to me immediately—pull up work package tracker for data migration, and let's see how things look there."

Mike went into AMIGO and pulled up the query to see all of the data migration project work packages by their status.

"Ah-Ha! Take a look here! See all these design work packages waiting for approval?" Jonas asked.

Mike nodded.

"Some of them have been sitting here ten to fifteen days waiting for design signoff. I'll bet you a cup of coffee that this team's project plan is slipping because they are paying for a bunch of their offshore resources to be developing these integrations, but no one has signed off on their design and authorized the development work to begin. If memory serves, AMIGO has timer functionality that allows you to set an approval clock for every work package, and if that approval clock expires then the work package is automatically approved."

Mike was nodding vigorously now. "Yes, Carlos did mention that to me. At the time, I thought it was a little too hasty and that there would be some pushback on using it. Now that I have some documented evidence as to the consequences of not using it, I will work with my PMO and advisory board to institute the use of that functionality."

"Excellent. Now you have one more team that is in the red right now— your procure-to-pay/supply chain team. Let's look under the hood and see what we can find."

After going over the other red teams, Mike was getting a grasp of Jonas's analytical pattern. He looked at the issues log and didn't find anything material. He then checked out the work packages and deliverables and didn't find anything material there. He looked at the team's resource capacity and schedule to see if there were any bottlenecks, and again nothing was catching his eye. He then went and looked at the key decision log.

"Bingo, I think we got something here, Mike. Take a look at these three key decisions around inventory management. These have been open for more than thirty days each!"

Mike clenched his eyes in frustration. "I've should have caught that myself. I was reviewing our key decision log last night, and I saw a bunch of key decision titles and descriptions, but no owners, no dependencies, and no targets. That's probably one of the root causes as to why some of the other areas on the program are treading yellow, too. We need to do a better job on our follow-through in this area and getting the right people to own these key decisions."

Jonas smiled encouragingly. "I agree, Mike, but look at these three key decisions in particular. They all have Joe Dombrowski, your VP of Operations, as the owner. This is one of those situations where you need to use your leadership skills to 'influence up.' One of my suggestions in preparing for this conversation is to lay out the facts of the situation, show Joe—through the data—the impact that the lack of decision making is causing the program, and go over what steps we can take to have this come to a positive closure as soon as possible. It probably wouldn't hurt to have a conversation with Charles to get his perspective as well; maybe even have him in the room when you have the conversation."

Mike grinned back at that idea. "Yeah, I think that's a terrific idea. Thanks, Jonas."

"Any time."

CHAPTER 20

Quality Management

A few weeks had gone by, and Mike found himself sitting in his office, reviewing the latest critical chain heat maps and team status reports. By enforcing some new disciplines around issue management, key decision documentation, and turnaround, and putting a five-day timer on all documents that needed approval, there was a renewed "program focus" that was enabling the teams that were tracking red to become the more appealing colors of yellow and green.

Mike was actually feeling pretty darn good until an email popped up on his computer from Cheryl Crocker, head of internal audit. He opened up the email and starting reading. Cheryl said they completed their assessment and wanted to have a meeting to discuss their findings and their recommendations to beef up some quality assurance aspects within the program.

Mike had scheduled a meeting with Jonas to go over a few things, and he was confident that with some tips from him, he'd be able to address their quality management concerns.

Jonas knocked and then entered, looking cool and confident despite the summer temperatures. "How are you, Mike?" he asked as he sat down and placed his laptop case beside him.

"Doing well, Jonas. Yourself?"

"Good. How's your family?"

Mike frowned for a moment, debating how to answer. "Nancy is about to start her radiation treatments," he finally said. "Some people said it'll be hard, but only in comparison to those who haven't been through chemo. Next to chemo, this should be a breeze."

"Did I ever tell you my wife is a survivor?" Jonas asked.

They'd casually talked about Nancy's cancer battle, sometimes over meals or other times outside the office, but Mike was sure Jonas had never mentioned that his wife, Karyn, had fought cancer. He shook his head.

Jonas took that as an invitation. "Fourteen years ago, now," he said, taking out his computer and speaking without making eye contact. Mike was glad; there was a part of him that really hungered to hear a success story. It had been many difficult months for his wife and for their family. And for himself.

"She was diagnosed with a Stage II cancerous growth in her right breast. Family history and all that, so she elected for chop-chop." Jonas made it sound like it was no big deal. "I remember her telling me, 'Kiss them goodbye—they tried to kill me!'"

"Double mastectomy?" Mike said, whistling. "Wow. At the same time?"

"Heck no," Jonas replied. "A few months apart." He regarded Mike for a moment with a steady gaze. "Anyway, I know this is personal talk on company time, but I just wanted to say from one husband to another, you've done a good job. You've had a hard challenge, the transformation and being there for Nancy, and I think you've held it together really well."

"Thank you," Mike replied. It was odd how much hearing that from Jonas meant to him. "That means a lot."

"So, you didn't call me here to talk about our wives' deadly boobs?" Jonas asked with a twinkle in his eye.

Mike barked a laugh. "No! Quality management. I re-read your prep kit[14] over the weekend on quality management, but I thought maybe you could give me a deep dive on it. We're having some issues."

"So, you've already stepped in it?"

---

14 For more information, go to www.platinumpmo.com/thetransformationbook

"Afraid so," Mike said with a grimace.

"Okay," Jonas said, thinking for a moment. "Would it help if I talked to you on how I usually build quality into the digital transformation programs that I have run in the past and see how closely that matches up to what you are doing now?"

"Definitely."

"I want to show you a quality assurance model that encompasses four facets of digital transformation: project management, change management, solution management, and services management. I can also provide specific details about review, validation/verification, reporting, and advisory services that need to be considered to prepare the course for a successful digital transformation."

"That sounds perfect, Jonas. Thank you."

"Any time."

Something unspoken passed between the two men. They both understood and read between the lines and then moved on.

"So how do you know if your digital transformation program is going well," Jonas said rhetorically. "How do you measure quality? You know all the stats on the higher costs, overruns, and failures of transformation initiatives. But when I was when doing some research a while back, I ran across a study that suggests that a contributing factor to failed transformation initiatives is that the appropriate quality assurance activities were not defined and reported, resulting in the statistical cost overruns, system performance deficits, and/or failure to achieve the expected benefits. This demands we ask *how* our program is being run and that we measure the quality of the initiative."

"Right. It's not enough that they're just doing the work."

Jonas nodded and went on, "Digital transformations involve a transformative journey from the as-is state to the desired state. Business transformation to the to-be structure is accomplished through the implementation of changes in areas that span vertical and horizontal territories—and on multiple fronts, including people, processes, systems, and data.

"This requires a quality assurance initiative to identify key areas of your digital transformation program that can be compromised by failures in quality.

This initiative must also specify planned and systematic activities to provide adequate confidence that, when rolled out, your product will fulfill your organization's requirements for quality and achieve the envisioned business value."

"Right," Mike agreed. "We are getting some 'quality management' that is supposed to be coming from Gley & Stratton as part of our contract, but, according to our internal audit report, it is not hitting the mark. We have our external audit in a few months, and I do not want this to be a red flag on that report. Tell me more about your model and what you think we can bring into the program at this date to mitigate this risk."

"Well," Jonas replied, "let's get you up to speed, and then you'll know how to appraise their quality management. A good quality assurance model can help you to better understand the facets of your digital transformation and hence, achieve better control of your overall program implementation. The overall objective is to provide a framework that supports the quickest possible program deployment without sacrificing quality or functionality within the allocated budget. That is—the successful implementation of your digital transformation in terms of functionality, quality of service, schedule, cost, training, deployment, operation readiness, and post-implementation."

"So, what do you recommend for QA?" Mike asked.

Jonas answered, "My recommended QA model covers four facets of typical digital transformation initiatives that require quality assurance to ensure the successful completion of your program based on the critical success factors established at the beginning of your program. These areas are program management, change management, solution management, and services management.[15]

"As part of your quality assurance, your QA team, which I usually recommend to be an independent entity outside the program and organization, will provide the services of review, validation/verification, reporting, and advisory."

"Well, we have proven that doing this within the program has not worked for us so far, so I have to agree with you there," Mike told him.

----

15 "Quality Assurance Model Capturing ERP Implementation Facets through RVRA Services"; Jarallah S. AlGhamdi and Zeeshan Muzaffar; *Department of Information Technology, Ministry of Education, Saudi Arabia; Department of Information and Computer Science, King Fahd University of Petroleum and Minerals, Saudi Arabia; (jghamdi, szeeshan)@moe.gov.sa,* jaralla@kfupm.edu.s, ISBN 978-89-5519-154-7

Jonas made a noise in his throat. "Yes, I have seen that before. It's sort of like the fox guarding the henhouse. Although a firm's quality group is usually an independent group, there are typically some biases there because you are critiquing your own company. It is sometimes difficult to call out poor work on your own firm. That is why I recommend an independent firm with no other 'skin in the game' on your program.

"But back to your question—traditionally speaking, most QA initiatives fall slightly short by only providing review, validation/verification, and reporting services and leave it on to the solutions integrator or program leadership to make critical decisions for improving quality based on the feedback provided by QA. So, I recommend building a QA team that comprises experienced and skilled personnel that will look at your digital transformation initiative from different perspective (a QA perspective).

"I believe it's beneficial to seek advisory services from your QA team as well, not just their findings. This enables your QA team to provide useful advice and alternatives to your solution integrator and program leadership team to improve quality of your program and future solutions."

Program Management and Governance

Mike asked, "So what are we asking the QA team to review?"

"I recommend program management and governance, staff assessment, risk management, and program information/reporting," Jonas answered. "Do you want me to dig into that a little deeper?"

Mike nodded, so Jonas went on, "The goal of program management quality assurance is to provide effective monitoring and controlling of the overall program and the processes and tools used to govern the program. The QA team will use the appropriate tools and techniques to evaluate the program and processes based on the standards created for the transformation and report on the overall program status regularly.

"The purpose of monitoring and controlling is to ensure that the program is progressing on schedule and is delivering the required products while satisfying the acceptance criteria. In addition, the quality control assesses whether or not the program is staying aligned with the business case direction, and, if not, enables course correction if deviations are found. The QA team will analyze the governance processes around scope, change control, risks, issues, actions, and key decisions to ensure they are in line with leading practices."

Mike asked, "*How* do they do that, though?"

Jonas replied, "One of the tools the QA team should incorporate into their method is one we discussed before when we talked about surrounding qualitative program assessments, our 'seven keys to success' model.

"If you remember, this model uses a set of factors to consider while managing quality during your program. These factors provide an integrated framework that assess your overall program risk and quality, and assess the critical and often-conflicting demands on quality, time, resources, speed of delivery and cost containment.

"Since we already talked about implementing the seven keys to success into your program's operational cadence, this approach should be fairly easily adopted by your QA team. The additional value you will get from your QA team using this approach is an independent and objective perspective that you can compare to your internal assessments utilizing the same measuring tools."

"What about staff assessment?" Mike asked. "Is that the same?"

"Sort of," Jonas replied. "Staff assessment supports the solution integrator and the program leadership in interviewing and qualifying key resources assigned to the project by the solution integrator, any other third-party providers, and the organization itself. The purpose of this effort is to assess that *the right things are done*, that they are done *by the right people*, and they are done at the *right time*."

"All of those are good things," Mike quipped.

"Indeed. Two of the key metrics that will be used as part of the staff assessment are the issues log and the key decision register. These tools will be used to evaluate the staff that is driving the program by solving problems and making critical decisions. Assessments surrounding resolution velocity, cognitive biases as well as decision 'stickiness' (in other words, decisions that are not declined, reversed, or overruled) are taken into consideration. As part of the staff assessment, reports will be generated on the QA team's finding and the team will provide recommendations for improvements."

"Okay," Mike replied, nodding. "That makes sense."

"The QA team can also help with our old friend, risk assessment. The QA team will be evaluating your overall risk management process, the execution of that process, as well as providing an independent assessment of any risks on your risk register (or any risk they have identified as part of their assessment which has not been identified on your risk register) they feel put your program in significant jeopardy.

"They'll review, evaluate, and advise on risk assessment and mitigation plans submitted by the program, ongoing risk management performed by the program, periodically review the actual program risks, and raise undiscovered or undocumented risks against the program when necessary."

"But they can also report on information, right?" Mike asked.

Jonas nodded to Mike. "As part of this assessment, the QA team is looking at the overall information availability, distribution, and reporting that occurs during the program's daily, weekly, and monthly cadence. The QA team is looking at the availability and accessibility of program documentation, the standards use for documentation, the integration of the key information components across the program, the program's standard reporting cadence.

"From this analysis, the QA will provide performance reports that describe any circumstances which have caused or may negatively impact the program, its design, development, implementation, cost, or time for completion."

"Now, based on my objective assessment, I think you guys have done a pretty nice job in this area. Your processes look solid, the reporting and decision making you are doing as a leadership team has been pretty good, the operating meetings I have been to have been run very well and are value-added. Plus, you are using the AMIGO solution, which should be an auditor's dream come true because the platform provides immutable documented evidence of everything that is taken place within your program."

Mike began to chuckle a bit. "I know. I didn't want to interrupt your train of thought as you were going through the program management stuff. I wanted to hear if we were missing anything, and frankly, it sounds like we have it covered pretty well. In fact, it was one of the praises that we actually got on our internal report, but I just like to hear your passion on the subject," Mike said with a smile.

Change Management

Jonas smiled back at Mike and took his acknowledgment as it was intended. "Okay, Mr. Smarty Pants, let's go on to the next topic—change management. Did your audit report have any findings in this area?"

"A little bit. More questions around our approach than findings at this stage of the program. That being said, I know that someday soon, we are really going to start socializing with the whole organization on this initiative and preparing them for the changes to how they will work in the future. Shortly after we go live, Extron will be alone to live with our newly transformed systems—no more consultants—and our people need to be ready to stand on their own two feet. Doesn't quality control help with that expected changeover?" Mike asked.

Jonas said, "You cannot forget the effort needed to prepare your people for the change ahead. These are the activities to be undertaken by the change management team. Change management is a *huge* component of a digital transformation. In fact, one can argue it is the most critical facet of a digital transformation. As such, careful considerations should be established to ensure quality as part of your organizational transformation."

"For sure. What part does the QA team play?"

"I can give you a list; they'll:

▶ Review the change management strategy developed by the change management team, check alignment with business strategy and advise improvements where applicable

▶ Assess the change management plan

▶ Scrutinize the identification and appointment of change leaders

▶ Review the training needs assessment exercise and provide recommendations where applicable

▶ Analyze change communications and awareness campaign plans, check for alignment with the change management strategy and report findings

► Examine the feedback received as a result of change communication and present findings to the program leadership

► Review and validate training plans and knowledge transfer plans, report findings, and provide recommendations for
improvements.

► Assess deployment and operations readiness plans from a
change management perspective

► Evaluate the execution of change management plans and recommend improvements when necessary

"That's tremendous value from them," Mike commented as he considered Jonas's list.

"I am sure your OCM team from Gley & Stratton are covering a lot of the
things I just spouted off, but it is good to get an independent perspective from
professionals who specialize in this area just to make sure you have your bases
covered."

Solution Management

"So, did the audit report mention anything about the software development to
date?" Jonas asked inquisitively.

"As a matter of fact, it did," Mike replied. "A few of our auditors came
from other utility companies who have gone through a similar sort of implementation. They sampled some of our work packages and deliverables out of AMIGO
and provided some suggestions for improvement. They also had some concerns
about the number of interfaces we had to develop, where the data was moving
to and from, the type of data, and the what we were doing to secure that data
from outside threats."

"Excellent, those are some good questions to address," Jonas agreed.
Your quality assurance team can also help you with solutions management and
your digital transformation solution itself. They can help with solution design,
application development, testing, and data."

Jonas added, "As part of the solution design evaluation, your QA team will be assessing the quality of the following components:

▶ Review the application specifications and design documents.

▶ Validate the proposed solution against requirements and provide recommendations.

▶ Validate and review the solution architecture.

▶ Validate and review the design and implementation of security profiles.

▶ Validate the functional setup of the proposed solution in different environments.

▶ Ensure that the user requirements are reflected accurately in the specifications and design documents.

Mike asked, "What about application development?"

Jonas replied, "As part of the application development evaluation, your QA team will assess the quality of the following components:

▶ Review the application extension design and solution.

▶ Validate any customization against the clarity of code, the fulfillment of the requirements, and the usage of the recommended application APIs, database packages, and applications pack

▶ Review the proposed and implemented interface solution and provide a better solution in case of any glitches.

▶ Review the proposed and implemented reporting solution and provide a better solution in case of any glitches.

- ▶ Review the proposed and implemented workflows solution and provide a better solution in case of any glitches.

- ▶ Review the proposed and implemented mobility solution and provide a better solution in case of any glitches.

- ▶ Evaluate the results of the functional test and validation against any customization, interface, or application extensions.

"And based on the report, I'll probably want them in on testing, too," Mike thought out loud.

"I would. The QA team can:

- ▶ Review test plans developed by the program team to ensure conformance with the business requirements, quality policies, procedures, and standards. Because of their critical nature, special attention must be given to the system integration, performance, security, and user acceptance plans.

"Speaking of testing, if I remember correctly, AMIGO had some pretty robust testing functionality built into the platform?" Jonas said, interrupting himself.

"It does. What I really like is that it can take all the rules and requirements that were approved as part of our design and automatically populate our chosen test components for testing. This gives us an auditable traceability matrix to make sure we account for and test every rule and requirement in our system."

Mike went on to say, "AMIGO also has a pretty neat approach to building your test plans. You basically set up all of your individual test components, test cases, and test scenarios and set up some links between the ones that make sense into an overall test library. Then you use the AMIGO test plan builder to pick and choose which scenarios, independent cases, and independent components you want in your plan and the platform will automatically build your test plan for you. I showed this to our auditor, Cheryl, and she was very impressed."

Jonas replied, "That is great to hear, Mike. Testing is usually a dealbreaker for transformations such as yours. Sorry I went off on that tangent, but I wanted to be sure you knew about AMIGO's testing functionality. Let me get back to the rest of the quality assessment for solution management:

> ▶ Review the outcome of system, integration, and user accep-
> tance tests conducted by the program and end-user community
> and report exceptions and trends.

> ▶ Confirm and review comprehensive tests against application
> functional setup and security setup.

"And then it's time for data migration." Mike had heard this could be a difficult step. Without good quality assessment, he hated to think of what could happen.

"As part of this effort," Jonas responded, "your QA team will review and validate data conversion strategy, standards, and programs. They can validate the completion of data migration and full data load. And they can review the outcomes of the transformational error reports, the load error reports, the technical reconciliation reports, and user data validation results conducted by the program and end-user community and report exceptions and trends."

Services Management

"You mentioned services management?" Mike prompted. "What role do they play there?"

"Services Management refers to the pre-go-live operational readiness assessment effort, as well as the post-implementation quality assessment," Jonas replied. "As part of this assessment, your QA team will be evaluating a variety of aspects of your program and the organization's readiness to actualize your digital transformation."

"Important stuff."

"Yes. This assessment is a 360-degree audit to check whether the associated environment and products are ready, and that processes and people are in place to manage, operate, and maintain the new product. The pre-go-live review requires QA to perform a health check for each functional area within your digital transformation scope, conduct an independent validation of the Program Leadership's assessment of the 'to-be' deployed solution, and recommend a 'go/no-go' decision."

"So, I'm looking to this review to consider people, site, IT infrastructure, and data readiness?"

Jonas nodded and added, "Not just that. They'll also be looking at:

▶ User accounts and security rights

▶ End-user training and user support structure, including a final assessment that verifies whether the end-users are ready to adopt the new processes and technologies

▶ Hypercare/post-implementation support readiness

▶ Fallback options in the event of unforeseen implementation issues

The post-implementation assessment health check covers three categories:

▶ Health, availability, and overall usage monitoring of your new solution. The health monitoring covers those parameters that indicate the quality of service, while availability monitoring provides information on the availability of resources. Together, they provide an efficient mechanism to determine the performance of the system. Usage monitoring helps in the analysis of the ERP system from a utilization perspective.

▶ Execution of new business processes by end-user community. Your QA team should perform an evaluation to measure the adherence to the new way of doing business and the execution of the new business process by the end-user community. Report findings and provide recommendations for improvements.

> ▶ Evaluation of key performance indicators. Your QA team should perform an evaluation of the key performance indicators that have been built into your data and business processes. Over time, the QA team will assess whether or not the business is getting the value that was established as part of the original business case.

Mike wanted to show off. "So, by utilizing your quality assurance model and four facets of digital transformation (project management, change management, solution management, and services management), the quality assurance team will be able to provide specific details to help me in all these areas."

"Yes," Jonas confirmed. "They can be an amazing asset for the review, validation/verification, reporting, and advisory services and recommendations that need to be considered throughout your digital transformation to ensure that your end product satisfies your needs."

"One last question: Do they have QA teams for husbands?" Mike joked.

Jonas got up, knowing their meeting was over. "If they did," he said with a fatherly smile, "I'm sure yours would look amazing. I'll see you tomorrow."

CHAPTER 21

Life Goes On

"**M**y job as your radiation doctor is actually to get you back into your life," Dr. Heaton had told Nancy when she began treatment. Thirty doses of targeted radiation followed, but they were the gateway to freedom.

Honestly, Mike thought it had gone about as well as you could ask for. While Nancy had some friends she'd made in treatment who got positively baked—like sunburn—Nancy's treatment went much more smoothly. The demands on their schedule that five appointments per week put on the family were tough, but with Anna's help, they weathered that pretty well. Thankfully, according to Nancy, the treatments were brief but uncomfortable.

She'd had her cosmetic surgeries to rebuild first; the skin couldn't handle being nuked if the plastic surgeon was going to use it to rebuild, and Nancy said that, at first, it was pretty awkward to have young male radiation technicians positioning her, topless, for her treatments. By this point, however, Nancy also said that she'd pretty much lost all modesty thanks to the cancer.

They'd started family counseling in the middle of all this (even though they'd had to skip sessions during radiation treatment). Mike didn't care for it much, but the boys really hated it—except not as much as Gabbi. Mike swore that it was like bathing a cat to drag their teen to the appointments. The only way they managed to get her to go was wrapping it up in Nancy's treatment and blatant bribery. And threatening her with rehab.

The boys typically went first and were asked to talk about how their stepmom going through cancer made them feel, which was a difficult conversation because both boys had barriers about sharing their feelings—if they even admitted they had them. Donny's autistic tendencies and MJ's ADHD made those parts of the session like pulling teeth, but differently than when Gabbi took a turn. Combative, abrasively sarcastic, and hateful, she had a difficult time getting any value from their times.

However, the therapist had said that she was familiar with this type of process and told Mike and Nancy to stick with it. So, they did.

The last few months had been a back-and-forth with Gabbi. She'd smell like weed but played it off as someone else's. Then she'd done really well—until coming home with alcohol on her breath another night. She spent a lot of time grounded but still found ways to get in trouble without Nancy being able to hound her day and night.

Through it all, Mike worked and tried to hold it all together, and, slowly, life went on.

CHAPTER 22

Knowledge Management

For over a year and a half now, Extron had been flooded with extra-warm bodies—hard-working resources who had done the work in the trenches for the company's digital transformation. However, Mike could see that the days of having their knowledgeable vendors and consultants—including Jonas and Carlos—was nearing the end. According to his forecasted budget, a good chunk of consultants would start rolling off right after the system integration test was completed, so their next hurdle would be ensuring that the critical knowledge of the new environment didn't leave with the vendors and that Extron's internal team would be able to support the new solution.

Mike and Jonas were already planning for that eventuality, and as Mike saw the reports moving along (and even though "stuff" was hitting the proverbial "fan" during their first system integration test cycle), he knew that he needed to get his head wrapped around knowledge retention.

He and Jonas had been talking about it off and on for a couple of weeks now and had been getting deeper into it during a series of meetings. Jonas was in full-on educator mode and was telling Mike, "That's why it's so important to support effective knowledge retention as well as have the tools to capture, facilitate, and maintain your digital transformation program knowledge."

Mike had needed to get out of the office so he could clear his head, and Jonas had come along to get his caffeine fix from SheBrews, the nearby specialty coffee shop Mike liked.

"You don't have to convince me," Mike replied. *"How* do I ensure that all the pertinent knowledge that is obtained during the program is transferred to resources within my organization and not going out the door when the consultants leave?"

"Well, that's knowledge management," Jonas replied, looking at the menu over the counter. "What do you get here?"

"Yes, I know it's knowledge management," Mike replied, slightly exasperated. His head hurt. Caffeine would help. "The mochas are amazing—just the right balance of sweet and strong."

They ordered and sat down. Absently, Jonas said, "So, you know knowledge management is the methodical replication of the expertise, wisdom, insight, and tacit knowledge of key professionals into the heads and hands of their coworkers. It's more than just on-the-job training."

Mike nodded. He'd come to understand that. "A lot more!"

"Knowledge transfer seeks to organize, create, capture, or distribute the know-how of the most expert individuals in a field, usually in the heads of your solution integrator or third-party consultants, and ensure its availability for your on-going sustain or harvest organization."

They got up to get their drinks, and as they walked back, Jonas said, "Digital transformation programs are so knowledge-intensive, and often they have high levels of complexity and risk. Both could be minimized by transferring valuable knowledge from the most experienced, high-performing individuals to others in an organization responsible for sustaining the current and improving upon your strategic initiatives in the future. When essential knowledge is captured and shared, organizations see improved results across the range of project metrics, including cost savings, time-on-task, error rates, and innovative solutions."

Mike frowned. "But what if you don't have an organization with a culture of sharing?"

"Your senior leadership has to set the tone, Mike."

"In my opinion, Jonas, I feel that my leadership has had a history of keeping things internal to their own business units and not sharing common knowledge. It's kind of created a culture of internal competition at times. We have had challenges in the past with some of our IT resources who have moved from one business unit to another. They are pretty much thrown into the deep end of the pool to figure things out on their own. Not a lot of documentation, or human support, either. It hasn't been good experience."

"So, with all of this evidence, why is knowledge management tradition-ally short-changed?" Jonas asked rhetorically. "Well, according to the research,[16] when organizations fall short of this more comprehensive knowledge transfer effort, the reasons are many but often relate to cultural issues. Many organiza-tions point to the fact they have higher priorities and also believe there is insuf-ficient recognition of the value."

Mike asked, "So, how do organizations overcome those barriers and embrace knowledge transfer as an important business capability?"

Jonas told him, "Research indicates that effective organizations focus not only on culture, but also on *leadership*—which means you—and, even more importantly, on *people* because knowledge lives in and is applied by them."

"What do you suggest we do?"

Jonas took a drink of his coffee, thinking. "When organizations have a culture that values knowledge transfer, they are far more successful at it. In a study I've bookmarked, a full 96 percent agree that a supportive organizational culture—alone or coupled with state-of-the-art knowledge storage and retrieval policies and technology—contributes to effective knowledge transfer." [15]

"With culture central to knowledge transfer, who sets the tone? Do I have to wait for someone above me to champion it?"

Jonas replied, "More than half of organizations name senior leadership as ultimately responsible for knowledge transfer. It's imperative to have senior leadership actively engaged in sharing and directing the importance of knowl-edge. Leadership sets the culture, and that culture should emphasize the skills of collective collaboration and communication. Regardless of a specific title,

---

16 "Pulse of the Profession®": Capturing the Value of Project Management Through Knowledge Trans-fer March 2015

most organizations that are effective at knowledge transfer have identified someone in the organization who is ultimately responsible for knowledge management, compared to those that don't do knowledge transfer well."

Jonas paused for a moment, considering. "Equally—if perhaps not even *more* important to having a culture that supports knowledge transfer—is the buy-in and commitment of an organization's *people*. They are the vital link."

Mike considered this. "Kind of a grass-roots thing?"

"Sharing begins not only with decisions about the kind of knowledge to capture—what is mission-critical in the present—but also what would have value and contribute to longer-range, sustainable success within your digital transformation program," Jonas told him. "Organizations must then identify who has the knowledge and provide the tools and resources to make the process of knowledge transfer as routine and easy as possible."

"I think we could do that," Mike replied. "How do you determine what needs to be transferred? There's so much!"

"For the different methods for identifying knowledge that must be captured, the program's project managers specify critical knowledge. This allows project managers to promote, and even demonstrate, the value of transferring knowledge and how it contributes to an improved project delivery process. With that support and insight, employees are more likely to recognize their roles and participate."

"So, I can help set the tone, but then it's the program's project managers who need to specify the critical knowledge," Mike repeated to himself.

"To help in this endeavor, your program management office can be a successful advocate for knowledge transfer. The most effective organizations are over five times more likely to have a PMO that supports knowledge transfer as a means of improving the management of projects and programs. They are also three times more likely to say that the PMO 'owns' the organization's knowledge transfer.

"You can use your program leadership to help advocate this cultural dynamic within your program and promote collaboration and knowledge sharing within your program's eco-system. As a program leader, you can incentivize your project managers to promote these behaviors within their project teams."

"Get them to buy in and own it," Mike mused.

"Exactly," Jonas commented, taking another drink. "By the way, you're right—this mocha is amazing."

"Chocolate and coffee," Mike said, toasting Jonas in the air with his cup. "Two good things that are better together.

The Knowledge Management Process

As the two gentlemen were enjoying their mochas, they noticed a familiar face at the register. "Hey, Carlos, why don't you come join us? We are talking about knowledge management."

"One of my favorite topics. I'll be right there."

Once Carlos sat down, the three of them began digging into the process of transferring knowledge. Jonas explained, "There are many ways for an organization to transfer knowledge. Some strategies will work better in one organization than another. The challenge is uniting the right steps, tools, and activities to transfer knowledge effectively. I found this process to be one that works well with large-scale, IT-enabled transformation programs such as yours.

"I think the steps of a knowledge transfer program—or the life cycle of knowledge transfer—involve identifying knowledge that is relevant and valuable, capturing and retaining that knowledge, sharing that knowledge with others, applying transferred knowledge, and assessing the value or benefits of specific knowledge."

"So, identify, capture, share, apply, and assess," Mike echoed. "I can handle that."

"I keep trying to make that into an acronym," Jonas said, "as though we don't have enough of those. But ICSAA just doesn't have a ring to it."

Mike shook his head and laughed, and Jonas went on, "Identifying relevant knowledge is essentially mapping its true value. Organizations need to—and should— know what knowledge aligns with their strategy and what they desire to be 'skillable.'"

"Word of the day—skillable," Mike quipped.

Jonas rolled his eyes slightly and went on, "One great method is to use your benefits case (or benefits realization plan) to drive the areas where knowl-edge transfer will provide the most value. Upfront, you should know how you are going to measure benefits and have built those mechanisms into your processes and data capture. As part of the knowledge management process, make sure you have people in place with the knowledge to make it happen."

"Who helps decide what's relevant?" Mike asked, serious now.

Jonas answered, "Project managers and project subject matter experts (SMEs) are the major drivers of identifying the relevant knowledge that needs to be harvested and transferred within the organizations. Once you identify the knowledge that needs to be collected, it takes disparate approaches to capture and retain that knowledge. One widespread guiding principle is to document lessons learned for each project or program. What you do with that knowledge once it's captured is equally important and can determine the success or failure of knowledge transfer."

Mike scowled. "So, don't mess it up."

"Don't mess it up. You need to know what to capture, when to capture it, and where to capture."

"Are some ways of capturing better than others?" Mike asked.

Jonas thought for a moment and then answered, "Some of the more common ways to capture knowledge include lessons learned/post-mortem/debriefings, subject matter experts, required documentation for project closure, the company intranet, knowledge transfer workshops, and mentoring."

"Mentoring?" Mike asked. "I knew we were paying you for something! But which is best?"

Jonas didn't bat an eye. "Organizations typically use multiple approaches, which I think is because doing just one or two things is not enough. Other activ-ities that are not as widely used but are more unique and innovative include critical incident reviews, case studies, interactive web-based material, database construction, knowledge champions, communities of practice, and dedicated knowledge transfer teams."

"It just seems like so much data to handle," Mike observed darkly.

"It is," Carlos interjected. "Which is one of the reasons AMIGO is so special. It is designed to be the one place you need to capture and maintain this knowledge. A place where all aspects of the program from day one are systematically captured and harvested for future use. This approach is a great way to mitigate risk for when your solution integrator and third-party consultants walk out your door with all of the knowledge.

"Even with a solid knowledge transfer program in place, it is nearly impossible for your sustainment team to retain all of the knowledge that is transferred. That is why you need a systematic repository to digitally retain all of that knowledge, one that your team can go back to as a reference and go through the history of the decision making, review the contents of the documents as to why things were built the way they were built, and use that knowledge as the catalyst for the ongoing process improvements that will continue once you have ramped down your formal digital transformation program and put your product into the hands of your organization."

"So, once you've captured your knowledge, you've got to share it?"

"Nearly seven in ten organizations report that they make knowledge available to others. This step has the highest percentage of organizations performing it, but their approach is different, as is the definition of what it means to make knowledge 'available.'"

"It all depends on what your definition of 'is' is," Mike joked. "How do most do it?"

Carlos let the comment pass. "The most common ways knowledge is shared include intranet search engine, peer-review process, informational networking/outreach, and post-implementation reviews."

"But I'm guessing not all of these are created equal."

"Right," Jonas followed up. "How organizations share and access relevant knowledge is a factor in their level of knowledge transfer effectiveness, which likely translates to project success rates. That's because not all methods or resources of sharing knowledge achieve the objectives of knowledge transfer; they don't necessarily engage people in a meaningful way. This is especially true if the only approach is the use of passive knowledge repositories. Organizations that are effective at knowledge transfer create a more interactive process that facilitates direct, person-to-person knowledge transfer."

Mike asked, "So is that the best? Person to person?"

"I agree that direct, person-to-person knowledge is one of the better—if not the best—forms of knowledge transfer. However, a major concern is the information overload that comes with knowledge transfer and your recipient's ability to retain all of that knowledge. It's like drinking from a firehose. That is why I recommend that, in addition to the bits and bytes knowledge transfer of the key specifics of the program, the knowledge transfer agent also transfers knowledge about the knowledge repository in which all content for the program is stored."

"AMIGO."

"Exactly," Carlos replied. "By having familiarity with this system and comfortably being able to navigate through the repository, your knowledge transfer agent is essentially teaching the knowledge transfer recipient 'how to fish,' thereby providing your recipient access to all the knowledge captured throughout the journey of your digital transformation implementation."

"Then, if they go, the recipient knows where and how to find answers," Mike said, understanding why Jonas felt this was so important.

"It's not just the knowledge," Carlos emphasized. "It's the systematic approach to capturing knowledge and knowing how to recover it. It's why AMIGO was designed to not just house the information but also have a mechanism to easily retrieve pertinent information and push specific knowledge to specific resources in a timely fashion.

"AMIGO's method is ideal for capturing as part of the repository you used to run your program. By using the human face-to-face elements of the capture process, along with the digital content repository, you are providing your organization a complete history of your program, along with the lessons learned for not only your sustain organization to continually improve on your digital transformation product for years to come, but as a mechanism for future programs to leverage the lessons you learned to avoid some of the challenges you faced during your journey."

"So, years from now, Extron can apply what we've learned during this process."

"Yes," Carlos agreed. "After organizations make knowledge available to others, the application of transferred knowledge follows, which is often a challenging step."

Mike asked, "What makes it so challenging?"

Jonas responded, "Technology is frequently used to facilitate applying the knowledge that has been transferred. But it's important to remember that technology is most effective when it's used to *aid* the people, not to *replace* them. I know some people in the artificial intelligence space that disagree with me, but there is still most likely going to be a human element long after your digital transformation goes live."

"So, you don't think we'll all be replaced with robots anytime soon?" Mike asked with a laugh.

Jonas broke into a big grin and shot back, "Well, maybe *you*, but you will find that when your program ramps down, there are certain members of your program that will continue on the journey as part of your sustain or harvesting organization. These team members will be the conduits of your program to the newer members of the sustain organization. Use these resources as your human engagement to the past to help position your sustain organization for the future support and evolvement of your digital transformation product.

"And that just leaves the hardest step—assessing."

Mike asked, "Why is assessing the hardest?"

Jonas considered his answer for a moment. "It often is, but it provides the biggest payoff. You need to determine the mechanisms to measure success. Assessing the benefits of knowledge is where organizations struggle. In fact, only 27 percent even make an *effort* to determine the value knowledge transfer delivers. Many find the value difficult to measure, because it's not always tangible or precise. The majority of organizations that are most effective at knowledge transfer measure project success rates to determine the value of their knowledge programs, whereas other organizations question whether the correlation is direct enough to assess."

"Which makes me wonder if they didn't have a very good systematic process in place. Maybe they *can't* assess it very well."

"Indeed," Jonas replied. "A great way to measure the success of your knowledge transfer is to tie it to your overall benefits realization plan because knowledge is a variable in the value you are getting from your digital transformation initiative."

"So, you really can assess it at the end," Mike commented, finishing his drink. The caffeine and sugar had recharged him, and he felt like he had a really good handle on the information, thanks to Jonas. "It sounds like knowledge management is an ongoing and evolving process of learning, adjusting, and improving the results of your program's efforts."

"I hope you can embrace the value of sharing knowledge and strive to make it a 'norm' within your organization," Carlos replied, quickly downing the last of his espresso. "AMIGO was designed to provide the right blend of technology and human engagement to get the most value from your knowledge transfer efforts."

"It'll pay off," Mike predicted.

Jonas came back, "You know this—knowledge is power, and transferring that knowledge is a powerful aid for the successful sustainment of your digital transformation initiative and for future digital transformation programs to come."

"Hey, do you guys have time for another cup of coffee? There something else I wanted to talk to you about while I have both you and Carlos at my disposal."

"As long as you're buying," Jonas said with a smile. Carlos just nodded and looked meaningfully at his empty cup.

CHAPTER 23

Program Integration

"**S**o, we've talked a lot about the integrated core," Jonas mentioned, "but while each of the components is separate, in reality, they need to work in harmony with each other. You might not know it, Mike, but you have been doing it already. It is called program integration."

"Yeah, it probably doesn't do a lot of good to have a good handle on all these separate things if we can't put them together," Mike agreed.

"It's the role of the program leader and the program management office to establish an environment where all of these components are captured, reviewed, measured, verified for deficiencies and anomalies, and corrected as part of an ongoing operating rhythm throughout your digital transformation implementation journey."

"I think we've done a pretty good job at this so far, correct?" Mike asked inquisitively.

"You have. As you have already figured out, a critical component to this is to have the right tools in place to capture the content of these components, integrate them, and provide pertinent intelligence on the cross-impacts they have with one another. This, along with the creation of a program operating rhythm and cadence to measure, verify for deficiencies and anomalies, and take corrective actions is what program integration is all about."

"I get that," Mike said quickly. "AMIGO has been a tremendous asset in helping us manage the hundreds of spinning plates we have going all at the same time and showing us the integration impacts through its AI messenger. It really has been a godsend."

"Definitely," Carlos added. "AMIGO's program integration management involves the tools and techniques to collect, measure, validate, and advise on all of the processes required to ensure that the projects under your program are properly coordinated and working together. It involves driving open opportunities to closure and the delicate balance of making trade-offs amongst competing priorities, objectives, and alternatives to meet or exceed your stakeholder expectations while maintaining your triple constraint of scope, time, and budget."

"You're preaching to the choir, Carlos!" Mike jokingly said.

"I know, I know—but as you can see by the amount of gray on my head, I've been around the block a few times, and when it comes to this business, I've had lots of experience doing it the hard way," Carlos commented. "Earlier in my career, I was on a few very large-scale transformations at Gley & Stratton. We had some really smart people who had prior experience implementing solutions similar to some of the ERP processes we are implementing here today. They came with deep industry experience, solid technical skills, and very good soft skills, as well.

"We also had our excellent methodology and a way of running programs that generated thousands of documents from business process mappings, functional requirements, technical requirements, data mapping documents, training documents, testing documents, cutover documents, you name it. And all of these documents were stored on a file server or a SharePoint site, and there were probably five versions of the same document stored on five individual PCs, all of whom thought they had the master copy or latest version of the document. You can see how problematic that all was."

"Seems like it would never work," Mike commented. "Impossible to manage effectively."

Carlos just shook his head. "We made it work, but it wasn't efficient, that's for sure. And it took a ton more resources to make it all happen. We used to have issues lists, risk registers, actions list, and key decisions that were all captured on Excel spreadsheets and posted to SharePoint. That was as good as it got."

"Sounds pretty limiting."

"It was," Carlos confirmed. "Even today, there are folks out there that use either Excel or—if they are really sophisticated—MS Project to build project plans. And if their project managers are using MS Project and because the rest of the team does not have access to MS Project, their project managers will send out requests via emails for updates, get those updates back via email, update their plans, convert those projects into Excel, and distribute the team results via email—does that sound familiar?"

"It does," Mike said, shaking his head ruefully. "It's insane when you say it like that."

"I hope I am stirring up some negative thoughts," Carlos said, "because that is how most programs still run today. Right, Jonas?"

The older man nodded.

"There are great people with great skills," Carlos continued, "but they are stuck using the same tools to run their programs that were used when I was first starting out in this business in the early 1990s. The folks who built AMIGO decided that this industry needed a digital transformation for your digital transformation. You need a toolkit—actually, you need a platform—that allows you to capture and maintain all of your program documentation, program planning and execution, and governance actions in one place. And this platform should actually integrate all of the components of your program and provide you intelligence, down to the work package level, on possible disconnects and breakdowns within your program and provide alerts to the resources responsible, accountable, consulted, and informed on those components so that they can work together to resolve those disconnects. AMIGO does all that."

"It is your job as a program leader to make sure that all of these components of the transformation are working together in harmony," Jonas added. "In today's world, it takes on average fifteen to twenty resources to coordinate all of this kind of activity on a large-scale global digital transformation effort, and the information would still be *wrong*."

"Just think about what ten, fifteen, or twenty consulting resources cost you per year," Carlos commented. "It's a significant price tag to have a bunch of people running around trying to collect and manually tie information together. It's a lot of wasted money with limited value in return. That is why you need a digital transformation implementation platform to do this work for you with systematic and integrated accuracy."

"And that's AMIGO," Mike filled in. Jonas and Carlos nodded. "Thanks, Carlos."

"Any time. That's what 'friends' are for," Carlos added with a wink. "I need to head back to the office now. Thanks for the coffee, Jonas. I'll see you guys later."

PMO Operating Rhythm

"So, you've mentioned an operating rhythm or cadence a few times," Mike said to Jonas. "What do you mean by that? And are we doing that now and I just don't know it?"

"You are to some extent, but there may be a little room for improvement. Hear me out and let me know what you think.

"A program operating rhythm is a set of pre-defined processes of communications and interactions that should be present between different decision-making stakeholders to ensure that the flow of operations within your program is not interrupted and is controlled as intended. Having a solid, engaging operating rhythm provides you a math equation where 1+1=3."

"I don't understand," Mike admitted.

"In other words, you get more value from the groupthink of the decision-making community than making decisions or solving complex problems independently. Once you have established your program rhythm, which will include your program's project managers, you want that same rhythm to cascade down your project levels—effectively creating individual project operating rhythms that mimic the cadence and energy of your program operating rhythm."

"All right," Mike said. "So, the whole is greater than the sum of its parts.

I can get that. What types of communications and interactions are you talking about?"

"You might start with annual program planning for the overall strategic planning of your program (if it's a multi-year program) and/or for your overall portfolio to establish the programs you want to initiate, modify, or remove for the upcoming year. These are usually off-site conferences over a couple of days that you have with your executive leadership, decision review board members, and program leadership team."

"We had one of those at the beginning of the year."

"Right," Jonas confirmed. "The annual leadership summit. Another meeting you will want to have is a quarterly review meeting. This meeting is usually a one-day, offsite meeting with members of your executive steering committee, decision board, and program leadership to perform a rear-view mirror assessment of how the program has been operating to date, as well as determine a forward-looking planning session to address any course corrections based on any factors that have arisen since your annual planning session.

"Similar to the quarterly meetings, you want to have monthly meetings. They follow a similar agenda, but they are at a lower level of detail and a little more tactical in nature. These are usually one-day, on-site meeting with your program leadership and your project managers."

Mike thought for a moment, "I guess we have been doing portions of these. We do have a lot of meetings. We just never formalized it into an official cadence where we are forming a rhythm of communications."

Jonas nodded and then added, "Next, you have a series of weekly meetings. This is where your operating rhythm really kicks in, as it is the core cadence for your program and where the most interaction and consistent communications happen week in and week out. The weekly meetings usually have your Program Leadership, project managers, and possibly team leads based on your discretion.

"Finally, there are the daily huddles. If you are a scrum or agile person, these are your daily standup meetings. Here is where your individual project teams are going through what they plan to accomplish that day and what impasses are impacting their ability to move forward."

"We have some of these things in place but not all. My fear is if we add any more meetings, when will we get anything done?" Mike asked wryly.

Jonas answered back in the same dry tone, "When your meetings are properly held and add value, they are actually accelerants to getting things done." He cleared his throat, raising an eyebrow as though asking Mike if he could continue now. "I can provide a monthly operating calendar. These are the things that not only form the rhythm, but they also help keep the program on task. They'll fill a lot of your time, but your primary concern is keeping all these pieces integrating smoothly—and this rhythm will aid that."

"I see the need, I just hate meetings," Mike quipped. "Seriously, though, I get it—but any tips you may have on how to make this all work are welcome."

"Tips?" Jonas asked. "Gladly." He thought for a few moments. "If you are not doing it already, I suggest you recruit executive leaders to engage in the program and dialogue and keep them on board. Try to establish guiding principles to outline goals and objectives. Build functional teams with leaders representing each part of the company to encourage collaboration. Establish a robust governance structure to track progress and drive cross-functional decision making. Share leading practices to encourage continuous improvement. And celebrate success!"

"You've talked about sponsors before," Mike noted.

"Yes. Every program needs a champion, and you have one in your CFO, Arthur Jonesborough—someone who will advocate for the program, understands its benefits, and can corral cooperation from change-weary managers and employees. An executive sponsor brings the vision and energy necessary to effectively instill corporate change. Fortunately, the enthusiasm level for your digital transformation is still pretty high, so you should be receiving a refreshing willingness from traditional line-of-business and C-level executives who have not always been present in other past initiatives. If you're not, get input from Arthur and Charles and utilize their clout within the organization to get the cooperation you need."

"That's a really good idea. I know Charles is 100 percent behind this."

"Arthur's buy-in is even more powerful," Jonas replied. "Now, I am assuming you have done this already, but if not, you'll need to establish guiding principles to outline goals and objectives with your executive management team. Have your considered principles like these:

- ▶ Preserve valuable elements of your organization's culture.

- ▶ Build a cohesive team that embodies our organization's core values.

- ▶ Ensure minimal disruption to the existing customer base across the product portfolio.

- ▶ Strive for best-in-class and adopt leading practices in terms of people, organization, systems, processes, and data.

- ▶ Complete our digital transformation within the commercial timeframe.

"Actually, Jonas, you'll be happy to know that we have, and a good portion of these are on our list."

"Excellent—your guiding principles outline the foundational roadmap and high-level goals that you are trying to achieve as a program and as an organization. When questions, critical decisions, and issues come up throughout your initiative, you can refer to these principles to ensure your actions and decisions align with your original objectives."

"It sounds like that high-level buy-in is pretty vital, not just upfront but throughout," Mike commented.

Jonas replied, "With your guiding principles at the forefront, keep in mind that a successful integration requires the support and dedication of all key players involved. You need to engage stakeholders from all parts of the organization who are within the scope of your digital transformation early and regularly to gain buy-in and keep things moving at the speed required."

"So, you're saying that a lot of my job has been and will continue to make sure that everyone is playing nicely together?" Mike asked.

"Time and people are the essence of the collaborative process," Jonas replied. "The process will reinforce core competencies, continue to build a forward momentum, and instill a collaborative approach towards your digital transformation. There's no doubt about it: Collaborative planning and execution are crucial to the success of your digital transformation program—and no, it's not just you."

"That's great information for the executive perspective the program," Mike commented, "but can we talk about the operational side? I want to make sure I am not missing anything in our current approach."

Jonas told him, "To ensure all planned tasks and work packages are completed on time and in accordance with the presented scope of work, you want to establish a comprehensive governance structure to track and report progress which, based on what I have seen so far, you have done a pretty good job."

"Thanks for the vote of confidence," Mike chuckled.

"I am hoping that on a weekly basis, each functional team is building their own dashboard from data pulled out of AMIGO and submitting it to the integration program management office, which details what the team has accomplished that week, highlight any risks or issues, and outline the key areas of focus over the next four weeks. This cadence allows your program leadership to review progress, discuss potential risks, and address issues in an organized and timely manner. In addition, every other week, the executive team meets to discuss the overall progress of the integration program and make any critical decisions in real-time. This robust structure helps maintain momentum as you execute your plan."

"That is kind of what we are doing to stay on top of this now, so I feel better."

"That's great. As you're moving through this cadence, always look for opportunities to improve the process and improve the rhythm. One thing I suggest is to look to your individual value streams and enabling streams that are experiencing success and have them share key learnings with the rest of your program so that other teams adopt their leading practices."

"To help make the others better."

"Right. Each week, in your check-in meetings with your value stream and enabling stream leads, discuss successes and challenges. Share common themes and leading practices to members of each value stream and enabling stream as part of a weekly report that measures progress.

"Sharing these leading practices fosters better and open communication, increases efficiencies and productivity, and promotes a culture of continuous improvement. In addition, the weekly report gives all the streams transparency into how the overall program is progressing."

Mike noted, "It seems like a good way to celebrate their success."

"You've heard me say how important that is. We all want recognition that we're doing a good job. The entire planning, governance, and execution process drives rigor and impeccable attention to detail and is essential for the success of a digital transformation initiative. All of your work packages, deliverables, and milestones are completed by a collective group of individuals who have come together to accomplish a strategic goal for your organization. At times, things are going to be overwhelming, especially when you are in the dog days of your implementation, so celebrating accomplishments is extremely important to make sure your program team feels their hard work is appreciated."

"I'd think that would elevate the atmosphere, too, and make a more positive workplace. What have you seen work well?" Mike asked.

Jonas thought for a few moments, then said, "I had one client, Heidi Summersville, who I thought just did a bang-up job in this area. She had a program 'all hands' meeting every Thursday morning before the consultants would start traveling back home later that afternoon. It was a great way to build unity and comradery across all of the moving parts within her program. These were usually very positive and upbeat meetings that lasted about thirty or forty minutes.

"During these sessions, she would usually do two things. She would first provide a topic of interest completely outside the program. This client happened to be a utility client as well, and, like you guys, health and safety were key measures for them and embedded in the culture. So, every week, she would pick something out of a journal on being healthy, exercise, good nutrition, proper sleep, personal safety tips, whatever, and gave an informed five minutes on something I personally would never have considered. I just thought it was a great way to bring community to the team."

"That's really interesting," Mike commented. "It probably helped everyone stay loose and to talk about something else for a few minutes. What did they do after that?"

"She would give a brief five minutes on the state-of-the-program and go over some of the highlights from the last leadership meeting that had just taken place. Then, each team had a representative who discussed the quick wins they had the week before and their overall game plan for the coming week. This was a great way to inform all the other teams about what every other team was doing to contribute to the success of the program."

"I'd think that would build comradery instead of competition," Mike thought out loud.

"You got it. She then set some time aside to give shout-outs to key members of the program who did special something the week before that significantly contributed to their team and the program for that week. It was a really nice 'thank you' and great motivator for your program."

"How big were these meetings?" Mike asked.

Jonas wagged his eyebrows at Mike meaningfully. "Roughly two hundred."

Mike's eyes got wide.

"You might be thinking that this is a very expensive meeting. Thirty minutes at a $150 per hour average cost for two hundred people—it's about a $10-15,000 meeting each week. Yes, that is expensive, but you have to think of it as an *investment*. An investment in building an engaged program. An investment in building individual teams that work together. An investment in reducing your program's overall risk by communicating weekly as a program and possibly identifying integration impact areas along away. In the long run, the benefits of this meeting far outweighed its costs."

Mike had to chew on that for a while. Could he justify such a meeting?

CHAPTER 24

Leadership Principles

As they walked out of the executive steering committee meeting later that afternoon, Jonas squeezed in beside Mike. "I like how you handled that," he said.

"What?"

"When John asked you that question, I thought you showed really good leadership skills. Is that something you've studied?"

"Leadership?" Mike asked. "Yeah, some. Enough to know that everyone has their own ideas."

Jonas nodded. "Don't I know it! For some, leadership is motivation; for others, it equals results, and for others, it is inspiration. If you Google 'what's leadership,' you're going to get millions of responses. But I think when you start looking at those responses and the undertones that follow, you'll find some core principles that resonate throughout each of those definitions."

Mike was headed to his office, and Jonas was following, so he knew he had a few minutes. "So, I'm curious, Jonas—what have you seen good leaders do in your digital transformation initiatives? I can manage the program and 'check the boxes for success,' but how can I effectively lead my team through all of the trials and challenges of a large-scale implementation?"

"That really is the challenge," Jonas confirmed. "Leadership and management are really different things."

They arrived at Mike's office, and he grabbed them each a bottle of water from his mini-fridge before they sat down. "I agree," he began, "but knowing which to do when seems like the difficulty."

"I like James Hunter's definition of leadership: 'Leadership is the skill of influencing people to enthusiastically work towards goals identified as being for the common good, with character that inspires confidence and excellence.'"

"I like that," Mike commented before taking a big gulp.

"As part of my research and my personal experience, I noticed some key principles that seemed to be in everyone's definition of leadership. I can share if you'd like?"

Mike glanced at his watch. He had some time. "Yeah, hit me," he said, leaning back.

Jonas smiled self-deprecatingly. "Okay, so I call it my *briefcase of leadership principles.*"

Mike's eyebrow quirked up, and he smiled at Jonas but didn't say anything.

When Jonas saw Mike wasn't going to comment, he continued, "There are the eight core principles that I have put into my personal leadership briefcase and that I try to utilize every day. Everybody matters. Get to know your team by letting them get to know you. Make yourself available to your team. Build trust. Be transparent and communicative. Be emotionally intelligent. Lead vs. manage. And finally, be a servant."

"A servant?" Mike asked.

"A servant," Jonas confirmed. "As simple as it sounds, you probably learned the majority of what it takes to be a servant leader while you were still in kindergarten: Always be nice, always tell the truth, do what you said you were going to do, and share. And then, when you got into second grade, you probably learned about the golden rule: 'Do unto others as you would have them do unto you.'"

"That's all I need to do?" Mike asked, laughing. "That sounds too easy."

Jonas shrugged. "What we tend to forget as we are moving up the professional ladder—or getting beaten down by the politics or bureaucracy within an organization, or striving to deliver a critical program—are the *human* aspects of what it takes to be a great leader. To me, it's stuff like being the boss you would want your boss to be, being the co-worker you would want your co-worker to be, and being the leader you would want your leadership to be."

"That's all pretty basic," Mike said, nodding.

"Yet these are the building blocks of good leadership. Everyone on your program matters, no matter what their role is. Even if they are not on your program and just part of the organization, they matter. Treat them with respect and applaud them for the value they bring to your organization. When I go onto a client's site for an engagement, I go out and look to meet a variety of people from all aspects of the program and beyond. I want to know the programmers, the organizational transformation team, the business process teams, the infrastructure guys. I even go as far as getting to know the people who take care of the plants and serve the lunches at my client site. At the end of the day, it is about building relationships and acknowledging each and every individual contribution to the greater good of your organization of the organization you are representing."

"It's easy to just think of leadership as the people directly under my authority," Mike commented thoughtfully.

"Don't just focus on building relationships with your direct reports or your executive leadership team. If you do, you will be missing out. Go out and build relationships with your direct report's direct reports. Go out and tell those people about the great things their bosses are telling you that they are doing and how valuable their contributions are to the success of your program. Be the mouthpiece of your executive leadership, and share the guiding principles of your program with everyone. Explain how your program ties to the organization's goals and objectives and how important each individual on your program is to making that happen."

Know and Be Known

"That sounds good, Jonas, but how do you even do that?" Mike asked.

"You have to get out of your office and walk around and get to know one another," the older man replied. "You might know everyone on your team, but what about your vendors? These people are going to be carrying out your transformation, and while we use the term 'resources,' they're definitely more than 'resources.'"

"You're talking about valuable time," Mike commented skeptically, shaking his head a little.

"You're right," Jonas countered. "Your time is valuable. So is theirs. Yet think on this: If your transformation initiative goes more smoothly because you've communicated effectively and know the strengths and weaknesses of your team, is that going to slow you down or speed you up on the back end of your program?"

"So front-end load getting to know them," Mike said, thinking it through, "and it saves time on the back end?"

"Definitely," Jonas confirmed. "As part of getting to know your team, first start out by sharing something about yourself. Share your personal interests, career aspirations, management style, or a little something about your family. Let them get to know the real you. This shows a little vulnerability, which is good. You want to be authentic. This will be one of the first openings to building a trusting relationship with your team, and hopefully, they will reciprocate and be as open and expressive as you were when you get to learn about them."

"So, just go out and walk around, talking to people?" Mike asked.

Jonas shook his head, "Not just that. Use technology to help bridge this gap. I highly encourage folks to build a personal profile as part of your program toolset. Think of it as a program Facebook page where folks can share this information with others across the team about their role in the program, their professional aspirations, their hobbies outside of work, their families, you name it. I believe AMIGO has these capabilities built into its user profiles.

"Now, this concept has gotten a little more challenging these days, especially in Europe with the new GDPR and a person's general data protection rights, so make sure when you are setting something like this up that the information you collect is not too invasive or crosses any personal data protection policies. We want to build internal program engagement—not data mining to exploit. If you set this up correctly, it can really help build a personal touch and provides you a clearer 360-degree picture of what makes each and every team member tick."

"Social media for the program?" Mike didn't know what to think about that. "We have a hard-enough time keeping people off social media without giving them an excuse."

"You want connections," Jonas countered. "You want a *team*. And you're the one who will initiate all this. I know this can get pretty hard. You are swamped day-in and day-out and getting pulled in a thousand different directions. But as a leader, you must find some time to walk the floors, say hello to your team, and show genuine interest in their well-being. Again, use technology to help bridge the gap.

"If you are going to do a walkabout, for example, to the data migration team area, why not look them up really quick and check out their profiles as a reminder of the families, upcoming birthdays, hobbies, and *most importantly*, their *names*. This will go a long way in having a face-to-name recognition when you have hundreds of people on your program, and you can recite something as simple as that. It goes a long way in building that relationship and trust with members of your team.

"And let your program team know of your open-door policy. Set some time in your calendar for anyone to come and meet with you to talk about what's on their mind. And if it can't happen at work, allow them to contact you after hours. Let them know you are there to help them be successful."

"Are you joking?" Mike asked. "I spend enough of my time at work as it is. Nancy will kill me if I started using personal time for work."

Jonas held up his hands, "I'm just telling you what you can do to build your team. Building trust takes time. I found that the best way to build trust is by first giving trust. It's kind of like those falls you see on television where someone falls backwards and trusts their friends or coworkers to catch them before they hit the ground. Be the person to take the fall first."

Mike was still chewing on Jonas' previous words. "So, initiate."

"Yes. Be candid about yourself. Share one of your greatest accomplishments that you are very proud of, as well as one of your most abysmal professional failures that comes with a key learning lesson. This will show your vulnerability, which is a key component to building trusting relationships."

"I have a few to choose from," Mike commented.

"Pick the funniest," Jonas offered. "Establish an environment of trust and protection so that your team can work outside their comfort zone because they know they have a safety net in you. This will allow them to make the tough decision when needed and take on additional risks because they know you have their backs."

Mike nodded, thinking. "So that *they'll* initiate."

"Indeed. Give them guidance and direction along with the responsibility and/or accountability to make it happen, and don't micro-manage them. Be their coach through the process, and don't do it for them. If they fail, help them through the lessons learned from the failed experience as a teachable moment."

"That definitely sounds more like leadership than management."

"It's all about communication and openness," Jonas told him. "Let your team know what is going on within the program, how their tracks of work fit into the big picture of the overall program, how they are tracking in relation to the overall big picture, and—if necessary—what they need to improve upon if they are falling short."

"I hate that part," Mike said. "I'm no good at that."

"Only the jerks like that part. So, give them hugs and spanks."

"Spanks?" Mike said, a laugh on his lips.

Jonas looked at him dryly. "Or, maybe a different term you may have heard is 'carrot or the stick.' Praise people when praise is warranted, and be direct with people when they are falling short of expectation. Sometimes, you just have to tell them that they are just not cutting it. Get it out and let them know, and then help them build a game plan to correct the behavior and let them know the consequences if things don't improve."

Mike grunted. "I know. I have had to have some of those conversations with one of my guys, Chet, of late. They are very uncomfortable."

"I know they're uncomfortable, but they're necessary," Jonas replied solemnly. He went on, "Next, as the late Stephen Covey used to say, 'Seek first to understand, then to be understood.' This requires that you listen first, understand, then communicate back based on your understanding."

"So, be an active listener," Mike interpreted.

"Yes. If you understand them, you can see *why* they're not meeting expectations. Then, if you can lead them to a better alternative, hopefully, they can turn things around and become a valuable asset to the team. It all comes back to using your authority and influence to help them—to serve them. Can I tell you a personal story?"

Mike nodded.

"So, many years ago I thought I was a pretty good program manager; well actually, I thought I was a really *really* good program leader. When, in actuality, I was just an okay program manager. You see, I was struggling with the development of my ability to influence others to want to follow me. Instead, I was using brute force to get them to do what I wanted. I found it very frustrating. I knew I knew my stuff, and I was very good at what I did. My clients were paying me a bunch of money, so why weren't they listening to me and doing what I told them to do?"

Mike's eyebrow rose as he listened.

Jonas went on, "I struggled with this for years, and then I got to a client where I saw an entirely different culture around their program. I saw folks who genuinely listened, respected one another, had constructive workout sessions to resolve conflicts, and truly demonstrated a 'one team' approach to the program."

"Sounds good. How'd they do it?"

"I sat down with my client's executive and shared my personal short-comings with him and asked him how he got his team to be like this. He told me that this was part of the organization's culture and was embedded in the principles of 'servant leadership.' In all honesty, I had never heard of the term, but I wanted to learn more. It just so happened that the organization was having a guest speaker to discuss servant leadership, and it was none other than James Hunter, the international best-selling author of *The Servant*. Well, I got to listen to James's lecture that day, and I was blown away. It really was a game-changer for me personally and for my career as a professional program leader."

"But I learned everything I need to know in kindergarten," Mike quipped.

"You joke, but really you're right. It's not hard—but we've often *forgotten*. Or we've learned the wrong leadership techniques, or we're trying to manage when we need to be leading as servant leaders. You've got to get inside their heads and hearts."

"But how do you do that?" Mike demanded.

"For years, our leadership principles tended to treat people from the neck down. You didn't want people to think and didn't care about their opinions; you just wanted people to *work*. Henry Ford was famous for saying, 'Why is it I get the whole person when all I need is a set of hands to do the job?' That is where we got the phrase 'hired hands.'"

"I did not know that."

"In today's world, neck down leadership no longer works. You cannot be a world-class organization or build a world-class digital transformation with a neck down mentality. The whole challenge of leadership today is how to get people from the neck up. Do you know how to get hearts and minds and spirits and creativity and excellence out of your team?"

Mike ignored that it was a rhetorical question and said, "No, that's why we're talking."

Jonas frowned but went on, "As a leader, you are your team's reality for half their waking life. If you are not leading them, if you are not creating a compelling environment, if you *don't get* it, you are going to lose them, and they will disengage."

"But how do I do that, Jonas?" Mike insisted.

"Basically, you have to ask yourself the questions that your team members are probably internally asking themselves:

- ▶ What's it like working for you?

- ▶ Am I going to raise my game working for you?

- ▶ Am I going to have a better career?

- ▶ Am I going to get promoted spending time with you?

- ▶ When I leave you, will I be better off than when we first met?

- ▶ Will you leave a positive mark on my life and career?

▶ What kind of environment are you creating for your people?

"It is your job, as a leader, to teach your team members about character, excellence, and service. Inspire your team to raise their individual games, inspire them to excellence, and get them to own it. Do that by modeling that for them."

CHAPTER 25

Developing Leadership

"I'm not sure I can do all that," Mike told Jonas, deflated. "I'm not sure I'm that kind of person."

As they talked about leadership, Mike saw within himself that, so far, he had been managing, not leading the way Jonas was describing it. He honestly thought he had the potential to do more, but it's like the secrets hadn't been unlocked yet. Talking to Jonas, he felt like the possibilities were opening before him.

"That's okay. Being a leader is a *developed* skill," Jonas told him. "There's no such thing as a natural-born leader. It's something you need to learn and need to practice. Is a two-year-old a natural leader? What is the human nature of a two-year-old?"

"Of course, they're not a leader," Mike quipped. "They haven't been through kindergarten yet!"

Jonas laughed. "Right. Everything you need to be a good leader, you learned in kindergarten. It's really funny and cute to act like a brat when you are a two-year-old, but it is another story when you are still acting like that as a forty-year-old. Mike, I've seen you in action. You're ready to take another step. Remember, just because a person is great at what they do doesn't mean they have the skills to *lead* others to do it. Think about it from a business perspective: How many times have you seen your best programmer asked to be a team leader and watch them fail miserably? Or your best sales generator asked to be the sales manager only to watch the division sales go down the toilet?

"Leadership is a *spiritual* quality—being able to capture hearts and minds and spirits and creativity and excellence. Vince Lombardi, the greatest NFL football coach of all time, said, 'Once you got someone's heart, the rest of him will go wherever you want him to go.'"

Mike took a deep breath. "Okay," he said finally. "So, I'm not sunk if I wasn't born with it. How do you capture your team members' hearts?"

"You have to learn how to. It is an acquired skill. First, you have to learn it, and then you have to practice it. Do you think a great golfer read a book on how to become a great golfer and *voila*, they became a great golfer? No—they read, they were coached, and they practiced and practiced and *practiced*. You have to intellectualize the principles and then practice these principles over and over until they are habitual and become part of your DNA—your character. Only then do you have the skills to be an effective leader.

"The key takeaway here is this: thoughts can become actions, actions become habits, habits become our character—and character becomes our destiny! Leadership is not an intellectual thing. You have to *do* something. Be intentional, and then measure your success."

Mike asked, "So, you're saying you can measure your leadership?"

"Yes," Jonas answered. "How many people are you going to hold accountable this week? How many crucial conversations are you going to have? How many people are you going to find to appreciate and give positive feedback to this week? You have to engage in the actions for them to become habits that you just do without even thinking."

Mike just sat there, soaking in what Jonas had told him.

After a few moments, Jonas continued, "Leadership is not about management, and it is not about your power. The late Ross Perot, a great leader and former presidential candidate in his day was quoted as saying, 'You want to manage something, go manage your inventory. You don't manage people, *you lead* people.'

"Leadership is not synonymous with management; leadership is synonymous with *influence*. People want to be inspired. They want to be around excellence, and they want to be around people with character.

"Leadership is not about power. There was a great quote by former British Prime Minister Margaret Thatcher some years ago when she said, 'Being in power is like being a lady. If you need to remind people that you are, you aren't.' I love that quote because people today should not be impressed by your title and power. They should be impressed by your passion, your character, your authority, and your influence with people."

"So, you're saying it's not about my power to get them to do their jobs right?"

Jonas shook his head. "Power is defined as the ability to force or coerce others to do your will (even if they would choose not to) because of your position or your might. Power does not give you excellence; it gives you compliance and broken relationships."

"I've never heard anyone talk about leadership like this," Mike confessed.

"Jack Welch, the great leader of General Electric in the 1980s, was quoted as saying, 'While everyone is looking up to serve the boss, they have their ass to the customer.' This type of behavior is incongruent with how it should be. How much wasted effort and energy is there in an organization that is kissing up to the next level of management? That kind of power mentality is toxic to an organization and toxic to your digital transformation program. It creates seagull managers and a low trust culture, which is extremely toxic."

"'Seagull managers?'" Mike asked.

"Seagull managers are those managers who sit at the top and poop on the ones below. They make it their personal mission to catch you doing something wrong. This approach is very hard on relationships and does not last long because the people that you value most on your program or in your organization simply will not put up with it and will leave. A good example of this is the former head basketball coach in Indiana, Bobby Knight. Bobby was a good coach, won a couple of national championships, but he was an absolute tyrant. He definitely treated his players from the neck down and was a seagull manager. Although he was there for over twenty years, he was ousted as a nearly disgraced coach for his leadership style and how he handled his players. This is what a power culture produces; is this what you want to be?"

"No."

Jonas leaned forward. "Power damages relationships. Power breeds compliance. It does not breed excellence, creativity, or passion."

Love and Authority

"That," Mike began, "goes against everything I've ever thought. So, what *do* I do? If I'm not leading from a place of power, how *do* I do it?"

"Authority or influence is the antithesis of power. That is what you want to strive for as a servant leader. You want to create and expand a circle of influence where people willingly do your will because of the influence you have over them, not your title. Power is something that resides in a company. Authority is something that resides in *you*. Something that you have created or given existence to. Something that you have 'authored.'"

"'Authored,' 'authority'—are they connected?"

"Authority is the skill of getting people to willingly do your will because of your personal influence. Gandhi, Mother Teresa, Martin Luther King Jr.—none of these great leaders had 'power.' They did not hold office, but they had great *authority*; they had global influence. Each changed the world based on their influence—their ability to get people to act according to their will."

"So how do you build 'authority'?" Mike asked.

"You *serve*," Jonas replied. "When you serve and you sacrifice, you build influence. Servant leadership is about serving and meeting the legitimate needs of others. And service is about *love*. Mother Teresa once said, 'Love has to be put into action, and that action is service.'"

Mike asked, "So I'm supposed to 'love' my team?"

Jonas countered, "How do you go about serving your team? How do you identify their needs to seek their greatest good? *Love* is about extending yourself for the well-being of another person.

"We serve by loving people."

"Okay," Mike interjected, "so I maybe haven't already heard all of what you're saying, but this 'love' stuff is losing me entirely."

"All right," Jonas said. "What about 'coaching'? Servant leadership is like coaching with care and compassion. Coaching is real-time. Servant leaders are engaged and coaching real-time. Coaching is about hugging and spanking—carrot and stick. Leaders are about motivating and correcting. It's about 'discipling' people to excellence. To teach them, to help them be the best they can be—to love them. *That* is leadership derived from authority."

Mike expelled a long breath. "Coaching. Loving. Okay—I can work with coaching."

"I know it's a lot to take in," Jonas conceded. "Think of your favorite coach from school. Did any of them just take you under their wing and mentor you?"

Mike didn't have to think long. Coach St. John, Mike's middle school football coach. He'd been an obnoxious, bald man with a drill-sergeant voice, but when Mike had been struggling with some troubles at home, he'd encountered a totally different side Coach St. John. The gruff, demanding man had been there for Mike when his own father hadn't been, and for the next couple of years, he'd loved Mike in his own rough-spoken way.

In that new context, Mike had eventually recognized that all of Coach St. John's work with them had actually been love—tough love, but love that pulled them together as a team and urged the most out of them. But he'd seen the kinder, more personal side of the man, too, and as he thought about it there with Jonas, he had the sudden thought that the man had likely changed the course of his life. Without Coach St. John making a personal investment in a directionless, hurting kid, Mike's life could've gone a very different direction.

"Yes," Mike told Jonas.

"I think good coaching follows the 'three F's,'" Jonas said.

Mike smirked at him. "You might need to explain that."

Jonas ignored Mike's expression. "First, there is foundation: You, as the leader, have to set the bar. What are the rules of the house? What does excellence look like? You need to remind people about this regularly. Second, there is feedback: You need to provide feedback to your teams. Positive feedback for the things that are going well. And finally, there is friction: You need to provide feedback for when things are not going well, and people are not delivering to the bar you have set."

"So, friction can be a good thing?" Mike asked.

"Indeed, it can. You need to hold people accountable to the core values of your program and organization. You need to build a culture where mediocrity is not acceptable. If you don't hold people accountable to excellence, then you are a thief and a liar to your program and organization."

"Wow," Mike commented. "That's strong language!"

Jonas shrugged and said, "As a program leader, you are being *paid* to hold people accountable. By pretending everything is okay and being everyone's buddy, you are just doing a disservice to your program and to your organization. It's the tough love a coach gives his team."

That made Mike think of Coach St. John again. Jonas went on, "If your people are not meeting the standards, you have to address the gap. You need to work with them to close the gap. And if they don't close the gap, then they no longer have the privilege of working on your program or within your organization. You cannot subject the rest of the team to mediocrity as it will end up destroying the team and your leadership. As a leader, you need to have the right people on the bus and in the right seats and the wrong people off the bus for the betterment of your entire team. Because the rest of your team deserves excellence, not mediocrity. Your team is not your greatest asset."

"So, what is?"

Jonas smiled as Mike walked right into it and said, "The *right* team is your greatest asset! As a leader, are you fielding the best team? Are you creating excellence?"

Mike considered that for a long moment. "So, by *not* making the hard call when people aren't meeting the standard, I'd be cheating the program and the company?"

Jonas nodded. "It is difficult but necessary. You demonstrate your character when you make those hard decisions. Character is about moral maturity and winning those battles between what you *want* to do and what you *should* do. It's what you do between the stimulus and your response. The thing that happens between a stimulus and your response is your character. If there is a negative stimulus, are you going to respond by blowing up (which is what you want to do) or by patiently and calmly addressing the situation (which is what you should do)? That is your character in action."

"I've never heard character described like that," Mike mentioned.

"When we talk about character in this context, we are not talking about your personality, we are talking about your substance, your values, your moral compass, your emotional intelligence, and how you respond to stimulus. It's a measure of leadership. I believe leadership is character in action. Leadership development and character development are one and the same. Want to be a better leader? Then you need to raise your character by doing the right thing even when you don't feel like it and being patient when you want to be impatient. Being kind when you are in a crappy mood. Appreciating people even when you don't feel like it. Listening to people when you're busy, holding people accountable when it's easier to just let it slide. You need to build that muscle of character, and that comes with practice."

"So," Mike said, thinking, "the only way to build character like this is by putting it into practice?"

"Precisely."

Mike was looking at his desk as he interpreted, "So, the only way to become a better leader is by leading."

He looked up to find Jonas regarding him carefully. "Earlier, you were demanding to know *how* to become a better leader," the older man said slowly, "but perhaps, you are seeing right now that you are *already* doing it—you're already building that muscle."

"On the job training," Mike commented.

Jonas nodded.

"Guess I'd better get back to it, then. Thank you, Jonas."

Jonas smiled his big smile, got up, and tossed his water bottle in the trash. "Any time, Mike."

Changes

Within a few months, and as they grew closer to the early testing phases, Mike had started to see a growth in Gina. With a decision-making system in place that Jonas had helped him develop, Gina seemed to grow more confident and understand when she had enough data and the responsibility to make a decision.

Mike would give Gina things to work on and suggestions, and she responded willingly. He came to appreciate that she was highly coachable. In fact, she blossomed so much in that short time that he soon put her in charge of the operational readiness project for their go-live.

Preparing the organization for the launch of this new digital product was such an important part of the process, and Mike believed that Gina had a good handle on how to get the organization ready to handle their new processes, technologies, and data. She proved to be a great champion for their business data efforts in the earlier phases of the program, and Mike could see all the hard work and effort she'd put in—empowered by some changes to his coaching—coming to fruition.

On the other hand, Mike had two additional conversations with Chet like the first. Chet always ended up saying that he'd work on it—that there wouldn't be any more problems. But the problems always resurfaced. Mike hated to think about it this way, but Chet's personnel problems began reflecting on his project's output. They'd lost Eirene—she said it wasn't Chet, but Mike thought differently—and the morale of Chet's people was low, and so was their productivity. Chet hoarded information to make himself a bottleneck. Mike was reminded of the factory analogy he and Jonas had talked about.

Mike finally admitted to himself that if Chet wasn't going to start helping the team, he was going to have to be off the team. And if that was his decision, then putting it off wasn't helping anyone. Reluctantly, Mike got up to go tell the man he'd come up with in Extron that he no longer had a job. Chet was in his office, working hard when Mike arrived. Mike knocked and stepped into the room.

Chet's face darkened. "More?" he simply said. "Can we just skip the dog and pony show? I'll work on it. But right now, I'm actually getting things done—*working*."

Mike let out a long breath. "Chet, I hate to say this, but it's time for a change. You're a hard-working, brilliant guy, but there's a level of excellence beyond your computer skills we need on this transformation. I need a leader in your position, not a worker. And I hate to say this, but I need to find that excellence from somewhere else in the organization. Thank you for your services, but they're no longer required."

"You're firing me?" Chet said, incredulous. "Who're you gonna get to replace me? Adhira? Good luck with that!" He banged his hands on his keyboard, disgusted.

"That, unfortunately, is no longer your concern, Chet. I wish you all the best in your future endeavors," Mike replied professionally.

CHAPTER 26

Implementation

Mike and Jonas arrived at Mike's office with fresh cups of coffee in their hands. They'd been talking about the final details of the implementation timeline, and Mike thought of a detail he hadn't shared with Jonas yet.

"So, remember when we talked about holding people accountable and not to be a thief to the program and organization?" Mike asked.

Jonas frowned a little. "Yes, that's always a difficult issue. It's hard to hold people accountable."

"Well," Mike said, exhaling a big breath, "I decided that if Chet Osborn wasn't going to close the gap for us, he'd no longer have the privilege of working on our program or within our organization."

Jonas' eyebrows rose. "I thought you said he was brilliant?"

"He is," Mike confirmed. "But he's also one of the most difficult people I—and the rest of the team—have had the unfortunate experience to work with. I talked to him about it so many times—gave him so many chances to start being a team player. He'd seem like he was listening, act like he was doing it, and then I'd find out he was just blowing smoke at me and hadn't really changed at all."

"That had to be difficult—letting him go."

Mike nodded. "I hated doing it. He is one of the smartest people I have ever met, and when in the right frame of mind, he provided amazing work. It was just that nine times out of ten, he was not in the right frame of mind, and the value he was providing just wasn't worth it anymore. As you said before, I need the right people on the bus."

"When you are building excellence for your organization, and you do everything in your power to help someone achieve that excellence, and they just don't get it, it is time to take them off the bus."

"Well, he's walking now," Mike said, trying to lighten the mood.

There was a gentle tap on the door. He was already up and just quickly opened it. Gina Paterno was standing there, her dark eyes bright. "Mike, are you going to join the operational readiness meeting?"

Mike reflexively looked at his watch. "Oh, thanks, Gina. I'd completely lost track of time." He glanced at Jonas. "Hey, is it okay with you if Jonas tags along for the meeting to listen in?"

Gina smiled at Jonas. "I have no problem with it."

Together, the three of them headed down the hall. Mike explained, "The system integration testing is turning the corner, and our new digital platform is really starting to take shape. Now, the focus turns to the final stages of getting the organization ready for the implementation. As such, I put Gina in charge of setting up the operational readiness program for the go-live, and she's doing a bang-up job!"

Mike was pretty sure she could hear him, but it wasn't going to hurt. The transformation in her confidence was nothing short of inspiring, and it had been a revelation to see her take on the additional responsibility and do so well for the program.

"She's worked with the project managers across all of the different projects and has developed a series of operational readiness scorecards to measure the preparedness of each component of the digital transformation," Mike went on. "These scorecards will be a measuring stick by which the executive steering committee will make their final decision on whether or not to go live with this new digital platform."

"That's great, Mike," Jonas affirmed. "It sounds as though you have a great process in progress for the implementation so far."

Mike fell in step with Jonas and lowered his voice. "I've been really impressed with how she has grown from a dedicated worker with little confidence and knowledge about digital transformations to a key go-to person who is driving a critical program function."

"It must be a very proud moment for you as a leader and mentor," Jonas offered.

A part of him wanted Jonas to see the fruits of his leadership labor. Mike smiled self-consciously, trying to shrug off the moment. To deflect, he said, "According to the timeline, we are five weeks away from the go-live date where we shut down the old way of doing business and start up the new way of running Extron. Over the next five weeks, there will be a series of go/no-go decisions based on the execution of our operational readiness and cutover plans."

Readiness

They filed into the conference room where they were holding the weekly operational readiness meeting.

"The organization transformation management organization, with the help of their consultants from Gley & Stratton, has spent months preparing the organization for this moment," Gina said proudly. "The communication's team planned and executed all the communications to all of the stakeholder groups, customers, and vendors through a variety of media channels and townhall sessions, telling them about all the exciting new things that will be arriving with this digital transformation and how it is going to catapult Extron as a leading utility for decades to come."

"How are they taking it?" Mike asked.

"Really well so far," Gina replied. "There were normal questions, but not much pushback."

"Great," Mike said. "We didn't do all this work to back out now." Scattered laughter greeted his comment from the people gathered in the room.

Gina went on, "The business transformation team has worked tirelessly with the organization's executive leadership to prepare them for leading this trans-formation and winning the hearts and minds of the business units they have been leading. They also built a business transformation change network of key team leaders throughout all the business and data process areas and facility locations that have the knowledge and passion to lead the organization and their facilities through the day-to-day operations of the business while using this new technology."

"That's great," Mike responded. "How's the training coming to run that day-to-day?"

"The training team has done an incredible job of building a variety of training materials using the latest techniques in adult learning, from traditional classroom training, to web-based, self-paced training, to the latest adoptions of micro-learning and 'knowledge as a service' techniques to train the thou-sands of Extron resources who will be impacted by this digital transformation. In addition to our internal team's educational efforts, the training team also built a learning game using Ringorang to engage with our more than one million cus-tomers on our upcoming changes and the new experiences they will get to enjoy in about five weeks. We have received very compelling engagement results, and customer feedback has been great!"

Mike applauded. "Outstanding work, guys! How are we doing on benefits case? Are we assuring our leadership that we're on track to deliver the original benefits we pitched when we first floated the transformation?"

Gina nodded. "The value management team has maintained the steady path of ensuring that everything that was discussed as part of the original ben-efits case for the digital transformation is mapped to the appropriate business processes and data elements throughout the technology, and that concrete per-formance indicators have been established to measure the perpetual value that the digital transformation will generate for Extron for years to come."

Mike looked to Jonas, as though saying, "*See what I mean? She rocks!*" Out loud, he asked, "Process readiness?"

Gina moved the meeting on. "The process teams market to opportunity, opportunity to cash, supply chain, and enterprise asset management are chomp-ing at the bit and are ready to go today. All of their business processes are fully documented."

"I bet they are," Mike said lightly. "Are they completely ready to rollout?"

"All of their work instructions for each business process procedure have been tested against the system configuration and have been embedded in the training materials for each of the representative job roles throughout the organization."

"What about the interim processes during the go-live period?"

"All of the interim process procedures to run the company during the three-and-a-half week cutover period have been documented, and the power users from the change network team have been trained on how to use them."

"How's our technology readiness?" Mike asked.

"The technology infrastructure teams are providing great reports. The system performance testing is still ongoing, but the initial results are well within service level expectations. They are still trying to fine-tune the database to make the information processing run faster."

"What about networks and printing?" Diana Lopez from IT was asking about this the other day.

"All of the network and network printing at all facilities have been completed with no issues reported," Gina answered. She went on, "Though it took a few iterations, I am happy to report that all integrated software applications have been tested throughout the system integration test and user acceptance test and have passed their tests."

"Terrific. How are we looking on data migration?" Mike asked.

"The guys at Covice have done a wonderful job of getting our organization ready for our data migration. Through a series of what they call 'mock cutovers,' which are simulations of the data migration portion of our cutover plan, they have been able to report data migration results above 99 percent for their last two mock cutovers, which is great news. For the one percent that still manage to fall out, our master data management team is ready to address the anomalies and are prepared to make those manual corrections with some additional tools provided by Covice during the master data migration portion of the cutover plan."

Mike queried, "So, we're almost ready for cutover?"

"As you know, Mike, our first dress rehearsal of the cutover plan went so-so." Some people in the room nodded; one groaned. She was putting it nicely.

"There were definitely a lot of lessons to be learned. We reviewed our cutover event journal from the first dress rehearsal and made quite a few improvements to our operating cadence, reporting, and communication processes. Though we had about 5,000 tasks in our cutover plan, we still missed a bunch of items in our cutover plan."

"What are we doing to address that?"

"This time, things are going much better. The people running the cutover plan have a better understanding of what they are supposed to be doing. Our cutover command center is running much more smoothly, and the hand-off between people and tasks have greatly improved. People are also getting used to the twenty-four-hour execution cycle. The data migration portion of the second dress rehearsal is scheduled to complete on Tuesday night, and we are scheduled to start the simulation of the operational shutdown, transactional data migration, and start-up activities of our new solution as part of the cutover plan on Thursday night with a target finish of Sunday morning at eight."

"Do we have the contingency in place?" Mike asked.

Gina nodded. "We also were able to complete the simulation of our contingency plan in the event that everything goes to hell in handbasket, and we have to abort the cutover execution and revert back to our current oper-ating model. We have also identified our 'point of no return' where—no matter what happens—we are not rolling back, but we will fix the problems and move forward."

"What about after go-live—what's that look like?"

"Our hypercare teams are in place for minute-one after go-live," Gina explained. "The help desk call tree is programmed to re-route calls to our hyper-care team that's involved in our digital product. The core team and the future production support team have been working together for weeks in knowledge transfer and preparing the production support team to take over daily triage of the application six weeks after go-live. During the first six weeks, they will be providing support for twenty-four hours a day using mixed teams of the core development team and the production support team."

Mike was taking it all in, but he wanted to know what her overall thought was. "So, how are you feeling about where we're at?"

Gina replied, "Right now, I am feeling pretty good about things, Mike. I know we will have some 'gotchas' when it is for real, but I feel that the team is prepared for that. Our mantra has been, 'Make this go live as boring as possible,' and with that, everyone has been very focused on knowing the plan, participating in the half-day plan walkthrough sessions, having their backups in place just in case, and having their triage teams ready in case of a catastrophic event. Everyone is nervous and excited at the same time. We feel ready!"

Mike smiled at Gina and the people assembled in the room. "Excellent work, Gina. Thanks for the update. You all have done an amazing job, and I'm glad to have you all on the bus—the team."

There were a few other items to cover, reports from a few other people, but after Gina's report, Mike was confident that those were formalities. He stayed focused, but for him, the meeting was done.

Half an hour later, Mike and Jonas were headed back to Mike's office, and Jonas said, "You know, Mike, I'm really impressed with your growth. You've taken on this role and done a wonderful job."

"Why, thank you, Jonas," Mike said. "I bet you say that to all the girls, you flatterer."

"Not really," Jonas said back, serious. "Honestly. I'm very proud to see how you've taken on the leadership role they handed you. I know what you've been dealing with at home—it can't have been easy."

Mike sobered as well. "It hasn't," he said simply.

Jonas reached over and patted Mike's shoulders in a fatherly gesture. "I know. I'm really proud of you, Mike. But not as proud as you should be of yourself. You've risen to the occasion."

Mike took a deep breath. "Well, let's not get too carried away yet, shall we? We haven't implemented the transformation yet."

"No," Jonas agreed, "not yet. But you've done your prep work. You're ready—or you will be. You've led this program team to the finish line. Now it's time to cross the tape. Finish strong."

"Right," Mike said, nodding. "Finish strong."

CHAPTER 27

Epilogue

From diagnosis until she was done with radiation, Nancy's cancer treatment had taken over twenty-two months. Much of that had coincided with Mike's increased role as program director for the transformation. With Nancy's mother, Anna, in the picture, Mike had more time to give the transformation the attention it required, but he also wrestled with guilt over this.

One amazing conversation with Nancy had given him a lot of peace, and he often went back to it in his mind. It was while she was recovering from a chemo treatment, and she had told him, "Mike, if you didn't provide for us, we couldn't afford the treatment that's saving my life. I hate it that you're gone so much, but if you weren't, we wouldn't make it. You do your job—and I'll do mine and get better."

Because of the raise, he was able to support them throughout the treatment process. He had a friend whose wife had gone through cancer, too, and it had driven them to bankruptcy. Even with their copay and out-of-pocket expenses and other costs surrounding Gabbi's recovery and Donny's additional therapy sessions, they were good financially. Mike was grateful for that.

He tried to make their time together when he was home really count. He downloaded a mindfulness app and practiced disconnecting from work when he wasn't there so that he could really be present with Nancy. He went to the appointments he could, and he took off time for her milestones no matter what, like ringing the bell. He took his vacation time, and they had a staycation at home.

It was difficult, in a way, because he had faced some issues that he would typically have run to work to get away from. He met with the boys' teachers, therapists, and other specialists and was a part of reviewing their educational plans. All of Donny's therapists felt he was making excellent progress and coming out of his shell. His academic plan had him on course to continue with his class, and he seemed happier with school than Mike could remember. MJ's ADHD was always lurking right under the surface, ready to spring up and consume a family moment, but he also was doing better. His teachers could tell that the program he was doing was helping, possibly in part due to him working out and lifting weights more regularly.

Things had gone from rocky to bottom-of-the-barrel with Gabbi before they started to rebound. One night, she simply hadn't come home, and they lost sleep all weekend looking for her. They'd eventually tracked her down through friends and found her stoned out of her mind. It was the last straw, and Nancy had sent her to a live-in program in another part of the state, far from the group friends who were giving her the drugs. It was incredibly difficult the first few weeks, but after the emotional pain of having sent her teenaged daughter away, things stabilized and actually seemed to improve.

Nancy's treatments impacted her so much, and no one really understood how much Gabbi's drama was affecting Nancy's recovery until it was out of the picture for a little while. They visited Gabbi as often as they could, and it was hard, but Mike could see that it was the right thing to do after the first few months.

With the boys under control and Gabbi at the live-in, things were quieter for a while in the Bennett household—as much as they could be with Nancy's treatments and the normal activities the kids were into. The pace picked up with daily radiation treatments—thirty of them—and Mike was again grateful for Anna being with them. But that burst of energy (Nancy wouldn't have appreciated the pun) was the final sprint to the finish line.

With Nancy's radiation treatment team, Anna, and Mike looking on with massive smiles, she rang the bell there, too, commemorating not just the end of radiation but the end of her oncology team's treatment plan. A few weeks later, Nancy breathlessly went in for another set of scans on a Tuesday—which she hated and needed Xanax to endure—and then they all nervously awaited the results.

And that's where they had one last speedbump.

At four in the afternoon on the Thursday after the scans, Anna texted Mike, "*Can you come home? Nancy got a VM from the oncologist.*"

A deep pit opened in Mike's gut. If it were good news, that would not be how he wanted to hear about it. Making a few quick excuses, Mike grabbed his things and raced home, breaking several traffic laws in the process but without consequence.

He rushed into the house to find Nancy in tears and Anna's face haunted. Nancy couldn't even tell him what was wrong, so finally Anna explained. "They called this afternoon. Left a voice mail saying that the doctor needs to see us tomorrow."

"Tomorrow?" Mike repeated dumbly.

Anna nodded. It took weeks to get in to see Dr. Bradley, so if they were calling right after the scans and getting Nancy in this quickly, it couldn't be good. Mike felt like he'd been punched in the stomach, like he couldn't get his breath. He just sat and held Nancy while she cried for a while, but an hour later, he found himself driving to get take-out Italian food.

"God, how could you let this happen?" he railed when alone in the car. He screamed it at the top of his lungs and, for the first time, felt his own tears flowing. He'd been strong for Nancy as he'd held her, but now, alone, they flowed. In the privacy of the car, he yelled and questioned and cursed, pouring out his fears.

By the time he picked up the Italian food, the curbside server probably thought he was crazy, his face red and tear streaked. She acted like she didn't notice, but strangely, Mike found that his fear and anger were spent as he drove back. A strange peace started to settle over him.

"We'll just do what we have to do," he said out loud to himself. Mike and

Nancy were both people of faith, and having vented his fears, he now prayed a different kind of prayer—a prayer of trust. Of faith.

By the time he got home, he felt his strength had returned, and he was able to lend it to his family. It wasn't like the fear was gone, but he'd dealt with it. It no longer owned him. He wouldn't let it own his house, and with an effort of spirit and will, he pushed the fear back from his family and served them by taking care of their needs.

The fear flared up again for Mike the next morning when he woke up and got in the shower. He shouted—mostly silently—and cried in the privacy of the shower and let the fear and anxiety flow away down the drain with the soapy water. By the time he turned off the steamy flow, he felt better—centered somehow. Stronger.

He took a personal day from work and took Nancy to the appointment himself, Anna in the back seat looking gray. Nancy had made her own peace, but she still looked terrified. Mike still felt the fear, but again, it had lost its power.

He found he was even able to joke and bring Nancy out during the drive. It wasn't the hollow, deflecting kind of humor he may have used before; it was something warmer, more genuine. It wasn't a function of denial or avoidance; it was him using the fact he'd dealt with his fear—again—and now was helping another with hers.

But the fear quickly got replaced with anger when they arrived at the appointment and learned that the voicemail that had so terrified his family was actually a misunderstanding. The nurse hadn't realized how her words could be misinterpreted; the doctor happened to have had a cancellation, which is why they could get in so quickly. She was all ignorant and bright smiles, oblivious to the pain and anxiety her careless words had caused.

When the doctor came in like nothing was strange, he said, "Well, great news. There's no evidence of cancer in your body."

"What?" Mike asked. "We thought..." If Mike had been another man, he might've punched someone or at least yelled at someone.

Nancy now found her voice. She proceeded to tell the doctor exactly what had happened, from the time they got the voicemail till the time they got to their appointment. "Do you have any idea what we've been through the last twelve hours?" she demanded.

Dr. Bradley looked at her blankly, still not understanding fully. The nurse had the sense to look ashamed, now understanding what her misleading words had done.

"Well," Anna said, interjecting, "the important thing here isn't what *didn't* happen—it's what he just said. Did you hear him? He said you're cured!"

"Cancer free," the doctor correctly quietly.

Being the cautious fellow he was, there was a little spot of "uptake" (whatever that was)—the doctor wanted to keep an eye on Nancy, but it might've been scar tissue, inflammation, or other benign things.

It didn't steal their joy. Nancy had beaten cancer. She was cancer-free! She'd run her race, and she had won!

The Bennett family was soon made whole with Gabbi coming home. Their problems weren't over, but they were *together*. They continued family therapy. Gabbi had a lot of trust to rebuild and enrolled at a new school. The boys still had trouble at their school. Nancy would need time to get her strength back. Mike still worked a lot and still wasn't sure what he thought of having Anna underfoot all the time—she'd stay another few weeks to get them back on their feet—but they'd come through the most challenging time of their lives in one piece. They were together, they were alive, and they loved each other. They could work on the rest.

They weren't the same; they were different. Transformed.

The Transformation

The transformation initiative at Extron rolled out with only one minor delay and was on budget. Mike had felt better and more confident about it as time went on, and was growing more and more confident in his leadership abilities. He found himself listening with more empathy and feeling better about his balance of work and home life.

One of the biggest things he took away from his experience, interestingly, was that as much as the Extron world—and the transformation in particular—depended on him, his family needed him even more. With the transformation initiative implemented, Mike started putting more boundaries on his work life, and while he felt he was still performing well, he understood that the fast track to promotion was no longer the most important thing in his life.

Making some conscious choices and being a leader at home as well as work began to transform his home life, too. He and Nancy started being more careful with their diet and started working out more. Mike had put on weight while working so much and eating poorly, and Nancy vowed to eat right and get back to her healthy weight. Together, they set goals, and using a few tips from work, Mike helped them ensure they met them.

Reunion

Mike saw Jonas again nearly six months after the transformation initiative had rolled out, and he was already well on his way to becoming a different man.

Mike happened to bump into him at Fat Guy's, the burger place. It was a weekend, both were dressed down, and Mike's pickup order for family lunch—a rare splurge on their new diet—had to wait while he caught up with his friend.

"Jonas!" Mike boomed, the other man holding up a milkshake guiltily.

Jonas held up a milkshake guiltily. "I was in town and just couldn't resist our tasty old hangout."

They shared a laugh.

"You look great, Mike. I see you dropped a few pounds. How have you been?"

Mike said, "I'm doing well, Jonas. I am so glad I ran into you. So much has gone on since you rolled off our program. We have been live for about six months now, and things are running very smoothly now. Our company has truly adopted what we have built. We are starting to see some return on our investment as well, and our leadership is very happy with that. I couldn't have done it without you."

"Ah, thanks to Mike, it was my absolute pleasure. Hey, how's Carlos and how is AMIGO working out for you?" Jonas asked.

"Carlos rolled off the program about a month after you did. He has become a good work friend. We even have become Facebook buddies. As for AMIGO, it continues to be of great value to us. We had a few people leave the program; some wanted to get into business operations, and others left the company for new opportunities. AMIGO has been a tremendous asset in getting the new folks we brought on to backfill the open roles up-to-speed. They were able to catch on and really understand what we built and the history behind what we did in a matter of weeks."

"I'm so glad to hear that," Jonas said. "I wanted you to have every advantage you could have. AMIGO's designed it to be the one place you need to capture and maintain this knowledge. It's a place where all aspects of the program from day one are systematically captured and harvested for future use. This approach is a great way to mitigate risk for when your solution integrator and third-party consultants walk out your door with all of the knowledge."

"Yes, it feels good to be standing on our own feet now," Mike said with a smile. Then he thought of something. "You know, I just wanted to thank you for something else, too. What you taught me about servant leadership has really changed my life."

Jonas looked a little surprised. "Well, I'm glad it helped. Extron is lucky to have you."

"I wasn't talking just about work," Mike replied. "I never thought that learning to be a good leader at work would help me at home, but applying those same principles with my family has changed my life."

Jonas's face changed. The look he had when thinking Mike was talking about work was fine, but his expression as he realized that Mike was talking about his home life made a very genuine smile blossom on the older man's face. "Mike, I knew you would learn the balance. Being a leader in your home is the most difficult place of all."

Mike nodded. Boy, was that the truth. "When I started applying what I learned from you and your leadership principles to my home life, it really transformed things," Mike told him.

"Pun intended?" Jonas asked, taking a drink from his milkshake.

"Definitely!" Mike laughed.

Closing Remarks

Do you know when you are watching a movie and you see the phrase in the initial title, "Inspired by true events"? What you just read was also inspired by true events over the course of more than twenty-five years of professional management consulting experience. Only the names and companies have been changed, as they say, "to protect the innocent."

The one thing that I want to point out that is completely real is AMIGO. Based on my more than twenty-five years of professional consulting experience and the continual learnings from my clients and associated system integrators, I became frustrated with the lack of innovation out there for guys like me in the profession of program leadership and program management.

Simply stated, for my profession, the shoemaker's kids have no shoes. In terms of program leadership and management, the industry pretty much uses the same tools and techniques to run large-scale global initiatives that I first used when I was starting out as a kid in this industry back in the early 1990s. The only thing that's changed is that we have moved our program documentation from a file server to SharePoint.

What our industry needs is a revolution—a completely different way to look at how we implement software. It needs an established set of core processes, delivery principles, and an integrated platform in which to manage the tens of thousands of connection points that occur during a digital transformation implementation that will allow us, program professionals, to consistently deliver excellence regardless of:

- ▶ Client

- ▶ Industry

- ▶ Value stream

- ▶ Software

- ▶ Technology

- ▶ Methodology

With the advent of digital transformation, I felt it was time that my profession had its own disruptor. And that's why I started Platinum PMO and built AMIGO.

Platinum PMO, at its core, has three service offerings:

- ▶ We provide digital transformation, program leadership, and program management educational services through our Platinum PMO *Learning Academy.*

- ▶ Through our Platinum PMO *Consulting Practice*, we provide program leadership, digital transformation strategy, independent advisory, program management office outsourcing, and organizational change management consulting services to our clients.

- ▶ And finally, our AMIGO platform positions us to truly disrupt this industry. With our cloud-based *Accelerated Migration & Implementation Governance Office*, you can plan, document, integrate, and govern every aspect of your digital transformation initiative. Our platform will pay for itself in months though administrative headcount reduction and project software cost reduction, and it will give you peace of mind as the one and only source of truth for all aspects of your digital transformation.

If it hasn't come across yet, the one other thing I would like to share with you is that I am *obsessed* with program leadership and program management.

At Platinum PMO, my partners and I have been running complex programs for over thirty years, and our passion for program leadership, especially ones that involve complex digital transformations, has never wavered. Each of us has looked at each and every client as an opportunity to lead by example with what we have learned and continue to embrace the new challenges that each client provides and learning from them.

We have taken the lessons learned, along with continual education, and come up with what we think are better ways to run digitally transformative initiatives. We can truly say we have an obsession delivering excellence to our clients.

We have spent the past thirty years perfecting our approach to delivering high-quality programs for our clients, and I want to share some of that with you and help make a positive impact on your digital transformation initiatives.

Please reach out to us at www.platinumpmo.com/letstalk and schedule some time for us to chat. We can evaluate your current efforts together and determine if there are any opportunities for improvement.

Thank you again for reading my book. I hope you found it "transformational"!

About Rick Catalano

Rick Catalano is the Founder and Managing Member of Platinum PMO, LLC, a software, consulting and education company helping organizations implement their digital transformation initiatives. As a Digital Transformation Delivery Executive, Rick has used his 25+ years' experience jumpstarting implementation success for mid-size to Fortune 500 industry leaders. His program and project management abilities have propelled the successful launch of dozens of digitally-enabled transformations for clients around the world– driving process improvements and profit growth

He has successfully led and implemented large-scale, multi-million-dollar global implementations including custom-built applications, systems integration across multiple technology platforms and change management. His industry expertise spans a variety of industries including consumer and industrial products, oil & gas, utilities, retail & fashion, aerospace & defense and publishing spanning the entire value chain.

As a program leader, Rick is known as a strong mentor and coach that will motivate his people to overcome obstacles. He brings out the best in his teams in terms of efficiency and effectiveness and has developed skills to handle the complexities of multi-location, multi-cultural global implementations.

Rick is also the visionary architect behind the state-of-the-art Digital Transformation Implementation Platform, AMIGO-- the all-in-one platform that connects all of the people, processes and functions a company needs to deliver their Enterprise Digital Transformations on time, on budget and with the value promised in their business case.

Rick has a Master of Science in Management Information Systems and holds accreditations from the Program Management Institute as a certified

Project Management Professional and Risk Management Professional as well as Digital Transformation Professional accreditations from CXO Transformation.

He is considered an outstanding program leader; a natural motivator and a change agent who strives to drive proactive transformation and achieve quantum leaps in productivity and efficiencies. Rick is a father of three adult children and resides with his wife, Cheryl in Hot Springs Village, Arkansas.

Made in the USA
Monee, IL
13 May 2021

68508127R00142